The Book

An actor's guide to Chicago

Edited by Carrie L. Kaufman

Published by Performink Books, Ltd.
Seventh Edition

PerformInk Books, Ltd.
P.O. Box 459
Flossmoor, IL 60422

ISBN: 1-892296-07-1

Carrie L. Kaufman, *Editor*

Arlo Bryan Guthrie, *Art Direction/Design*
David Stinton, *Illustrator*

All advertisements are published with the
understanding that the advertiser/agency has
obtained authorization for use of materials.

PerformInk Books, Ltd. does not take
responsibility for claims made by advertisers.

For advertising information, call 708 / 647-8100.

Table of Contents

A Checklist for Success

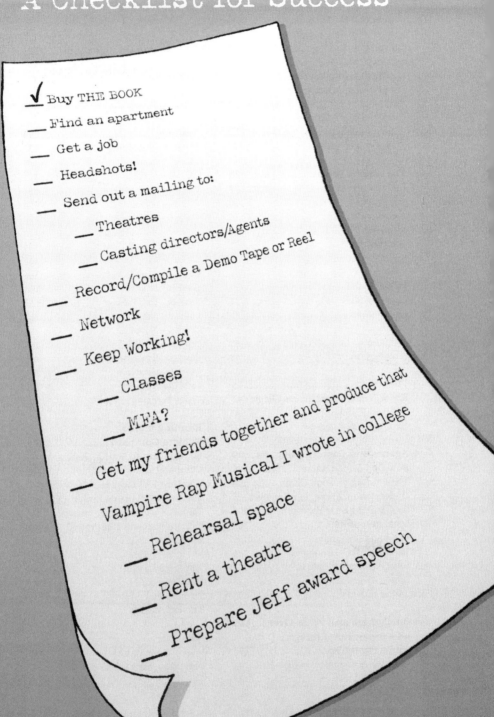

✔ Buy THE BOOK
___ Find an apartment
___ Get a job
___ Headshots!
___ Send out a mailing to:
___ Theatres
___ Casting directors/Agents
___ Record/Compile a Demo Tape or Reel
___ Network
___ Keep Working!
___ Classes
___ MFA?
___ Get my friends together and produce that Vampire Rap Musical I wrote in college
___ Rehearsal space
___ Rent a theatre
___ Prepare Jeff award speech

Looking for a Place to Call Your Own?

BY CHRIS GATTO

here is no surefire way to approach the housing quandary; however, a good method is to pick your neighborhood first. After you've put your bags down and caught your breath, you will be greeted by an amazing array of intricately interwoven and vibrant neighborhoods. Each neighborhood in Chicago has its own distinct personality.

To aid you in your search, we're providing you with some neighborhood profiles for areas throughout the city that are popular with actors and artists. In the following pages, you will find the most current information about rent rates, crime safety, and general neighborhood flavor. The rent information was collected from the CHICAGO READER (*www.chicagoreader.com*) and The Apartment People (*www.apartmentpeople.com*). Average housing prices come from *www.trulia.com* and the 2000 Census, which puts the prices a bit on the low side in today's real estate market. In the city, many housing purchase prices include condos.

The crime statistics were taken from the Chicago Police Department Web site. Please note: Violent crime "grades" given to a neighborhood include person-on-person crimes like assault, sexual assault, murder, battery, and mugging, while total crime includes that number plus things like vandalism, theft and arson. So if you see a neighborhood with an "A" for violent crime and a "D-" for total crime, you might assume that your body will be safe, but your property may not.

Remember, the profiles are intended to be guidelines, as neighborhoods are always changing. Most importantly, you need to go visit the neighborhoods that sound interesting to you. Make sure you feel safe, that the neighborhood meets your requirements for transportation and/or parking, and that the personality of the neighborhood suits you (not your friends). Here are some last tips to keep in mind:

- Visit the neighborhood during both day and night.

- Ask the people who live there—friends, acquaintances—what it's like.

- Do you need parking?

- Where's the nearest public transportation?

- Is there nightlife in the neighborhood?

- Will you like coming home to this neighborhood?

Other useful Web sites for Chicago neighborhood info:
www.cityofchicago.org
www.metromix.com
www.chicagoreader.com
www.apartmentpeople.com

It's a tall order, but don't be intimidated. The exciting part is that you get to experience all the diversity and cultural activity in the city, then choose where you will live. You make the choice!

On the Road Again

The Chicagoland interstate highway system has honorary names that designate an entire interstate, or a portion of one, or a merged combination of two or more. Although they can be confusing, these names are important to master. Here is a definitive list.

The Kennedy
Interstate 90 from O'Hare airport to the Loop (including the I-94 merge)

The Eisenhower
I-290

The Stevenson
I-55

The Edens
I-94 north of the 90/94 merge

The Dan Ryan
I-94 south of the Loop and part of I-57 (Note: expect delays as major construction is taking place on the Dan Ryan through 2007. For information, lane closings and alternate routes, visit *www.danryanexpressway.com*)

The Bishop Ford
I-94 south after the split with I-57

The Skyway
I-90 south of the Loop after 90 and 94 separate

The Tri-State Tollway
I-294

The Northwest Tollway
I-90 west of O'Hare, leading to Northwest suburbs

The North-South Tollway
I-355

The East-West Tollway
I-88 (starts where I-290 meets I-294, leads to Western suburbs)

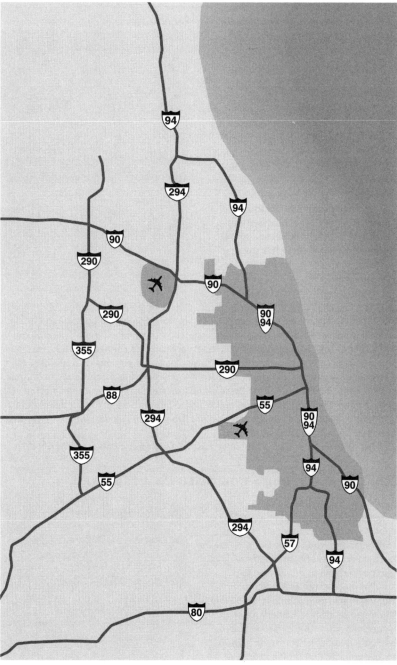

Chicago Interstate Highway System

What the 'L' ?

Chicago has a great transit system that is anchored by the 'L'—an elevated and underground train system. There are eight color-coded routes that can transport you to almost any destination you desire in the city, including both major airports (O'Hare and Midway) and some select suburbs. The Chicago Transit Authority (CTA) operates both the train and bus system (which is also quite extensive and user-friendly). Fares vary depending on payment method.

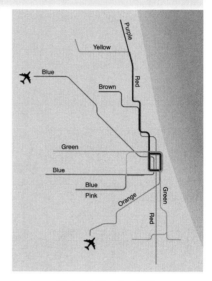

Chicago Card and Chicago Card Plus: Full fare is $1.75; transfer for 25 cents. Transfers allow two additional rides within two hours after the first boarding. Transfers from bus to 'L' or vice versa are accepted.

Transit Card: $1.75 on buses; $2 at rail stations; transfer for 25 cents. CTA Transit card vending machines are located at all 'L' locations.

See the official full-color CTA map on the inside back cover.

Cash: $2 per ride on bus and rail; exact fare only; no change returned. No transfers are issued when paying with cash. Turnstiles at rail stations do not accept cash. Customers must obtain a transit card from a fare vending machine at the station

It should be noted that the Brown Line (the train route that serves northwest Chicago into the Loop) is undergoing construction until 2008. Expect delays and temporary station closings when using the Brown line. The CTA Web site features extensive details on this expansion.

For more information, visit *www.transitchicago.com* or call 1-888/YOUR-CTA.

Metra—A Chicago Commuter's Lifeline

The Metra rail system connects Chicago to almost all its surrounding suburbs, and commuters swear by it. For under $10, you can travel from the farthest reaches of suburbia, as well as parts of Indiana and Wisconsin.

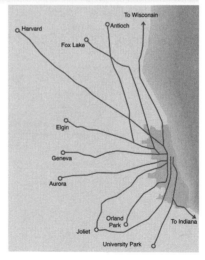

For more about Metra, go to *www.metrarail.com* or call 312/322-6777. The regional transit authority also has a special hotline that can help you navigate how to get from any point A to any point B. Call 836-7000, in any Illinois area code, for customer service.

Should I Own a Car in Chicago?

It's a question plaguing many city dwellers, but Chicago is especially unique because there are some places that are harder to get to without a car. But often it's easier to take the el or a bus. Decide whether you want a car or not before you pick a neighborhood.

Pros of Owning a Car:

• Groceries and children are pretty tough to haul on an el or bus.
• Marriott Theatre is in Lincolnshire; Metropolis is in Arlington Heights; Noble Fool is in St. Charles; New World Rep is in Downers Grove; First Folio Shakespeare is in Oakbrook...
You get the picture. There are lots of good theatres that are in the suburbs (where there are lots more audience members than in the city). You will need a car to get to most of them.
• You can live in neighborhoods that don't have an el stop and are usually cheaper because of it. Parking is usually better in these neighborhoods.
• You can go wherever the hell you want whenever the hell you want to.
• When it's January, you'll appreciate your heated car.

Cons of Owning a Car:

• When you get to where you're going, you have to find a place to park the #@!% thing.
• When you get home, you have to find a place to park the #@!% thing—and you usually have to pay for that.
• Many theatres in the city do not have parking attached and are in dense neighborhoods.
• Car insurance rates are much higher in the city.
• Plan on taking your radio faceplate with you; or having to replace the stereo and window at least once a year.
• Street cleaning (so they say).
• Go to Belmont Ave. on a Saturday night and watch all the people walking faster than the cars.

Pros of Owning a Motorcycle or Scooter:

• You can park in between cars.
• The traffic in Chicago doesn't go that fast, but you do have to watch for pedestrians.
• Insurance is pretty cheap.
• It's fun.

Cons of Owning a Motorcycle or Scooter:

• You can break you head—especially since you're not required to wear a helmet in Illinois.
• November – March. This chapter is not "Coming to Miami," it's "Coming to *Chicago*."
• Oh, and the children and grocery thing—it's a bit tough.

Andersonville

If you're looking for a cozy-but-in-a-hip-and-active-sort-of-way neighborhood, Andersonville's your spot. Otherwise known as Girl's Town, it's a popular stomping ground for lesbians and chilled-out gay men who can't keep up with the frantic pace of Boy's Town to the south. A family-oriented locale with an even mix of single-family homes, condos and apartments, the heart of Andersonville runs along Clark Street starting at Foster Ave. Historically Scandinavian, diversity is a hallmark of this tight-knit neighborhood, which houses large Asian and Hispanic populations.

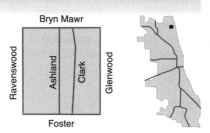

ACTOR BARS	Simon's and Konak
THEATRES	Neo-Futurists, Rogue Theatre
RENTS	Studio: $750 One Bed: $730–$1295 Two Bed: $1150–$2300
AVERAGE HOUSING PURCHASE PRICE	$284,178
CRIME STATS	Violent Crime: A Total Crime: A

Arlington Heights

Founded in the 1800s, the Village of Arlington Heights has preserved some of that old-world feel. In recent years the area has experienced a boom in economic growth and is easily accessible via the Metra. In the last decade, The Metropolis Center for the Performing Arts has become an alternative venue for Chicago theatres to transfer shows or do original work, so you could find yourself needing to get to the Northwest suburbs sooner than you think. Arlington Heights is also home to the Arlington Park Race Track and the Arlington Heights Memorial Library.

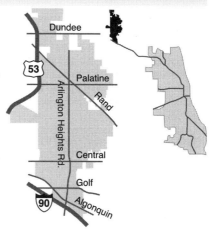

THEATRES	The Metropolis Center for the Performing Arts
RENTS	Studio: $750 One Bed: $730–$1295 Two Bed: $1150–$2300
AVERAGE HOUSING PURCHASE PRICE	$240,600

Bucktown

This is just your flat-out "cool" neighborhood with a touch of Bohemian flair. Over the years, Bucktown has transformed from an industrial corridor to a neighborhood alive with art, industry and commerce. Alongside Wicker Park, its sister-neighborhood-in-hipness, Bucktown is populated with cool clubs, night spots, coffee shops, bars and restaurants, and is a popular destination for young professionals and hipsters alike.

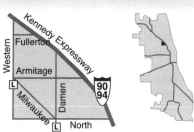

ACTOR BARS	The Bucktown Pub
THEATRES	Trapdoor Theatre
RENTS	Studio: $700 One Bed: $745–$1100 Two Bed: $1195–$2800
AVERAGE HOUSING PURCHASE PRICE	$462,728
CRIME STATS	Violent Crime: C Total Crime: B

Buena Park

It's close to Wrigley Field, but without the traffic. However, due to its proximity to the ballpark and large numbers of high-rises along the lake, parking can be a nightmare. Although not as attractive or lively as Lakeview, Buena Park still has reasonable rents and is public transportation friendly. The Gill Park District Building is used by many actors and improvisers for rehearsals.

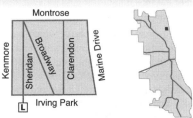

THEATRES	National Pastime, Mary-Arrchie, Strawdog, Profiles, Steep, and Oracle Theatre
RENTS	Studio: $525–$950 One Bed: $835–$1500 Two Bed: $1000–$1950
CRIME STATS	Violent Crime: B- Total Crime: A

Edgewater

Originally, Edgewater was settled by German, Swedish and Irish immigrants who carved out a posh residential subdivision for some of Chicago's most prosperous families and entrepreneurs. Today, it's a richly diverse community of working class families. It also attracts actors and artists with its low rents and easy access to public transportation. A car is okay in this neighborhood, but not necessary. Parking and driving can be bothersome, especially along the eastern edge of the neighborhood.

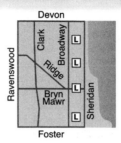

THEATRES	Raven Theatre, Actors Workshop Theatre.
RENTS	Studio: $475–$825 One Bed: $600–$1500 Two Bed: $1000–$1950
AVERAGE HOUSING PURCHASE PRICE	$284,178
CRIME STATS	Violent Crime: B Total Crime: B

Evanston

Just north of the city, Evanston is home to Northwestern University, which has cultivated a lot of Chicago talent and theatre companies. While some areas are very exclusive with mansion districts, the rents around the university and west of Ridge Ave. are quite reasonable. Overall, living here is generally more expensive than the city—and if you're in the buying mood, the taxes can total more than your mortgage payment.

THEATRES	Piven, Next Theatre, The Actor's Gymnasium and Piccolo Theatre.
RENTS	Studio: $660–$1400 One Bed: $700–$1950 Two Bed: $930–$2400
AVERAGE HOUSING PURCHASE PRICE:	$293,200

Forest Park

Forest Park is a fairly accessible suburb, both by public transportation and car. The blue line stops here, and the Eisenhower Expressway (290) runs right through it. It's a culturally diverse suburban area, adjacent to Oak Park. Parking is not a problem, as the majority of residences are single-family homes. (Note: This western suburb should not be confused with another to the south, the similarly named Park Forest.)

THEATRES	Circle Theatre
RENTS	Studio: $675
	One Bed: $725–$840
	Two Bed: $915–$1100
AVERAGE HOUSING PURCHASE PRICE	$143,140

Homewood-Flossmoor

The villages of Homewood and Flossmoor are two economically thriving and ethnically diverse southern suburbs. Recently named one of the best places to live by *Chicago Magazine*, the Homewood-Flossmoor area is located 40 minutes from downtown Chicago via the Metra. The park districts and the award winning education system, which houses the Homewood-Flossmoor High School, are a source of tremendous pride for the community. There is a significant, liberal Jewish population, and many residents work at the University of Chicago, just a 20-minute train ride away. Quiet and scenic, Homewood and Flossmoor preserve the ideal look of "Hometown USA," but with the feel of an artsy, liberal community.

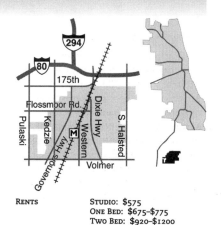

RENTS	**STUDIO:** $575
	ONE BED: $675–$775
	TWO BED: $920–$1200
AVERAGE HOUSING PURCHASE PRICE	$251,697

Humboldt Park

This largely Puerto Rican area is named for the beautiful park located in the middle of the neighborhood. The park itself is part of an intricate and vast boulevard system designed to link all of Chicago's parks from the north to the south sides. The park serves as a meeting and gathering place for events and recreation. Division Street, running through the southern end of the neighborhood, is known to the locals as "Paseo Boricua." It's a great neighborhood with vivid ethnic sights, smells and tastes; however, Humboldt Park still has problems associated with gang activity.

RENTS	Studio: $500–$600
	One Bed: $650–$750
	Two Bed: $700–$1850
AVERAGE HOUSING PURCHASE PRICE	$274,325
CRIME STATS	Violent Crime: D
	Total Crime: C-

Hyde Park

Hyde Park flourished as a neighborhood beginning in 1892, corresponding with the founding of the University of Chicago. The World's Columbian Exposition in 1893 further boosted development. The area is reminiscent of a quiet, yet busy New England college town and reflects the diverse lifestyles of the students, professors and professionals who make this their home. Streets are lined with old, shady trees, while block after block displays an incredible array of 19th and 20th century residential architecture—some of the most beautiful in the city. While the university serves as the anchor of

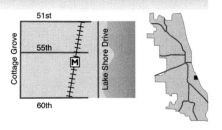

THEATRES	Court Theatre
RENTS	Studio: $650–$800
	One Bed: $875–$1200
	Two Bed: $1250–$1375
AVERAGE HOUSING PURCHASE PRICE	$302,387
CRIME STATS	Violent Crime: A
	Total Crime: A

the neighborhood, other sites and attractions are equally accessible, including the South Shore Cultural Center, the DuSable Museum of African American History and the Museum of Science and Industry. Once you've taken in the cultural ambiance, you can slip a bit northwest to US Cellular Field (also known as "The Cell") for a down and dirty ball game with Chicago's World Series champs, the White Sox. If the game isn't excitement enough, then maybe the fireworks afterwards will satisfy your entertainment needs.

Lakeview

There's always something to do in Lakeview—day or night. Late (and late-late) night bars, 24-hour eateries, Wrigley Field, diverse restaurants, coffee shops, vintage stores and a bevy of theatres are just a few reasons this area is so vibrant. Lakeview is a mix of young professionals, recent college grads and families. The rents definitely tend to be pricey; however, the saying "location, location, location" is very applicable here. Besides, it's always good to go where the boys are, and Chicago's definitive gay neighborhood—coined Boy's Town—is right here, running along Halsted between Belmont and Grace. Lakeview also serves as the central nervous system of the off-Loop theatre scene, with a slew of resident companies and shows in its vicinity. Still, keep in mind that because of all this wonderful activity, parking and traffic are generally *horrific*. Permit parking is in full regulation, but public transportation, thankfully, is plentiful and always accessible.

ACTOR BARS	The L&L Tavern, Town Hall Pub
THEATRES	Bailiwick, TimeLine, The Playground, Stage Left, The Theatre Building, Blue Man Group and Athenaeum Theatre
RENTS	Studio: $575–$1080 1 Bedroom: $745–$4525 2 Bedroom: $850–$4900
AVERAGE HOUSING PURCHASE PRICE	$224,797
CRIME STATS	Violent Crime B Total Crime: B+

Lincoln Park

Lincoln Park boasts one of the most desirable zip codes in the City of Chicago. That claim is arguable—depending on taste and yuppie endurance—but the area definitely seems to have population issues, as residents spill over into surrounding neighborhoods with cheaper rents.' The area is a mixture of residential and commercial zones, and is chock full of shopping, restaurants, bars and lots of single, beautiful people. It's also the home of DePaul University and Lincoln Park Zoo.

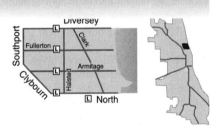

ACTOR BARS	The Red Lion (Chicago Shakespeare got its start here)
THEATRES	Victory Gardens (In their new space in the historic Biograph Building and with their Greenhouse space down the street), Steppenwolf, The Royal George, and The Apollo
RENTS	Studio: $460–$1329 One Bed: $600–$2584 Two Bed: $850–$4900
AVERAGE HOUSING PURCHASE PRICE:	$571,239
CRIME STATS	Violent Crime: C Total Crime: C

Lincoln Square

Lincoln Square is a homey German neighborhood that has become increasingly popular over the past several years. Overall, it's a diverse mix of Latino, Asian and Caucasian families; however, gentrification is hitting this area hard, making the formerly hidden gem increasingly crowded and expensive. Nevertheless, public transportation is good, and car parking is reasonable (for now). The Old Town School of Folk Music is located here.

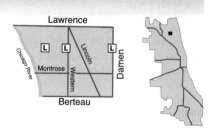

THEATRES	The Cornservatory
RENTS	One Bed: $745–$1600
	Two Bed: $810–$1800
AVERAGE HOUSING PURCHASE PRICE	$326,183
CRIME STATS	Violent Crime: A
	Total Crime: A

Logan/Palmer Square

This ethnically diverse neighborhood was originally settled in the early 1900s by poor immigrant tradesmen who gradually built prosperous businesses in the area. These "nouveau riche" also erected huge mansions in a mish-mash of architectural styles, many of which still compliment the neighborhood. Following in the eclectic heritage of the area, Logan/Palmer Square is extremely popular with artists. Gentrification is now driving up the price of living in some parts of the neighborhood. Still, it has retained an artsy feel and is very accessible by car and public transportation.

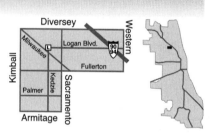

RENTS	Studio: $460–$1000
	One Bed: $650–$1025
	Two Bed: $650–$1995
AVERAGE HOUSING PURCHASE PRICE:	$334,531
CRIME STATS	Violent Crime: D+
	Total Crime: C-

Northbrook

This northern suburb is easily accessible by car and the Metra train. However, you need to factor in traffic when estimating travel time, which tends to grow exponentially during and around rush hour. The area is home to primarily high-income, single-family residents.

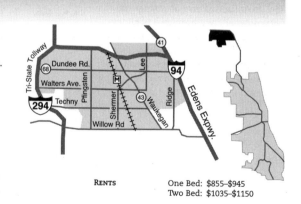

RENTS	One Bed: $855–$945
	Two Bed: $1035–$1150

Oak Park

This diverse community has a historic, yet progressive, feel—like many college towns. It has a prominent place in history, being famous for the architecture of Frank Lloyd Wright and as the home (although not birthplace) of Ernest Hemingway. Because of its close proximity to the city, easy parking and available public transportation, Oak Park is attractive to many artists and actors. Oak Park even has its own downtown area, which gives it a warm, hometown feel. Additionally, there is a large gay population residing in Oak Park; this suburb is one of the few communities in the country that gives domestic partnership benefits to gay spouses of city employees.

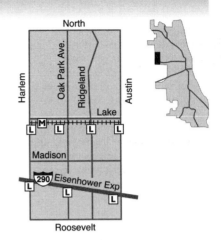

THEATRES	Oak Park Festival Theatre
RENTS	Studio: $575–$680 One Bed: $880–$1000 Two Bed: $1095–$1495

Old Town

Sandwiched between the Gold Coast and Lincoln Park, the historic neighborhood of Old Town is a treasure trove of pricey restaurants, upscale shops and bars. Originally settled by German immigrants in the 1850s, the area was virtually destroyed by the Great Chicago Fire of 1871. The buildings that survived—Victorian framed wood cottages and Queen Anne style homes—make up what is today known as the Old Town Triangle. The heart of Old Town (near Wells and North Ave.) lies close to the lake and adjoining parks, and it forms the theatrical epicenter of the neighborhood.

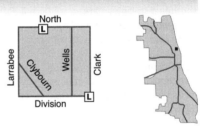

ACTOR BARS	The Old Town Ale House, Corcoran's
THEATRES	The Second City (featuring three venues: The Main Stage, The Etc., and Donny's Skybox), A Red Orchid Theatre, Zanies Comedy Club and the never-ending run of Tony 'n' Tina's Wedding at Piper's Alley Theatre.
RENTS	Studio: $975–$1100 One Bed: $1100–$1800 Two Bed: $1300–$3000
CRIME STATS	Violent Crime: C Total Crime: D

Orland Park/Tinley Park

These picturesque southwest suburbs, originally settled by Germans when Chicago was a young city, are now home to primarily upper middle class families. In 2005, Orland Park was named 45th in Money Magazine's "Best Place to Live in America" list. This list did not seem to include "traffic" among its criteria, as residents continue to complain that Orland Park's streets are congested from morning until night, due largely to the Orland Park mall and attendant national "mini malls" that line Highway 45. Tinley Park has seen a tremendous amount of revitalization over the last few years, as residents and businesses have worked to restore the downtown area to its historic glory. Metra travel is easy for both suburbs—The Rock Island District train runs to Tinley Park and the Southwest Service train has several stops at Orland Park.

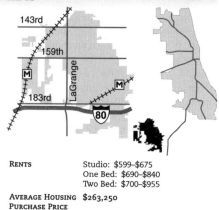

RENTS — Studio: $599–$675
One Bed: $690–$840
Two Bed: $700–$955

AVERAGE HOUSING PURCHASE PRICE — $263,250

Park Forest

This southern suburb is located off Interstate 57, southeast of Tinley Park and just south of Homewood and Flossmoor. The town was built as an incubator of progressive thought, and so it has a very diverse population—both racially and economically—and good public services. The population tends to be quite politically active, and very artistically inclined. The town has a comparatively low crime rate. Rents are pretty low, as are home prices, but there is no train stop in Park Forest. Residents will have to go north or west a couple of miles to catch the Metra Electric.

THEATRES — Illinois Theatre Center (ITC), as well as the Tall Grass Arts Association Art Gallery and School

RENTS — Studio: $545
One Bed: $599–$765
Two Bed: $775–$1000

Pilsen

Pilsen is truly an immigrant's neighborhood. Formerly the entryway for the Polish, Irish and Czech, Pilsen is now home to the largest Mexican community in the United States. According to Citysearch.com, the heart of the Mexican business community primarily runs along 18th Street, where taquerias, fruiterias and other small, family-owned businesses operate. The area attracts many artists with its rustic old warehouse and loft spaces; add to this tradition of activism and social reform, and a hotbed for artistic creativity is born. Somewhat accessible by 'L' and car, Pilsen is anchored by the University of Illinois at Chicago on the north side. Crime can be a concern, with gang activity still reported in this area.

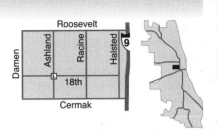

RENTS	Studios: $425 One Bed: $650–$900 Two Bed: $700–$900
AVERAGE HOUSING PURCHASE PRICE	$405,755
CRIME STATS	Violent Crime: B Total Crime: C-

Printer's Row/South Loop

Like many of Chicago's neighborhoods, Printer's Row started out as a bustling industrial area. It fell into ruin and neglect for a period of time before its current era of revitalization. This neighborhood is close to everything; it's very popular with young professionals working in the Loop, and the neighborhood reflects the tastes of those residents. Additionally, students attending nearby Columbia College and Roosevelt University live in the area. Easy access to Printer's Row is provided by public transportation, as well as by car via Lake Shore Drive and nearby expressways. Culture is close—just a short jaunt to the Adler Planetarium, the Shedd Aquarium, the Field Museum of Natural History and the Art Institute. For sports fans and outdoors enthusiasts, Soldier Field and Grant Park are at your doorstep.

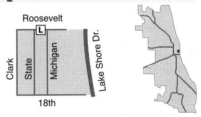

THEATRES	Goodman, Chicago Theatre, Gallery 37's Storefront Theatre, the LaSalle Bank Theatre (formerly the Shubert), the Ford Center/Oriental Theatre, the Cadillac Palace and Silk Road Theatre Project all reside in the nearby Loop area.
RENTS	Studio: $725–$1000 One Bed: $1025–$1850 Two Bed: $1400–$4500
CRIME STATS	Violent Crime: A Total Crime: A-

Ravenswood

In personality, Ravenswood has a similar feel to Lincoln Square. Originally settled by German immigrants, the area historically has been working class, although recently it has become a haven for increasing numbers of young professionals fleeing the crowds and high prices of trendier neighborhoods to the south. Still, Ravenswood maintains a family feel ensconced within tree-lined streets. Public transportation is easy and parking isn't a complete nightmare, so going out and about in this neighborhood is not prohibitive. Lastly, the rents are fairly affordable, but are rising with gentrification. GreyZelda, Remy Bumppo and few other theatres have their rehearsal and office space housed in the warehouses of this area.

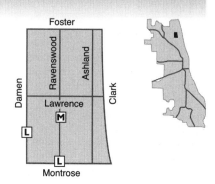

RENTS	Studio: $600–$750
	One Bed: $750–$975
	Two Bed: $875–$2200
AVERAGE HOUSING PURCHASE PRICE	$454,939
CRIME STATS	Violent Crime: A
	Total Crime: B

River West

This neighborhood is aptly named, as it is situated just west of the Chicago River. Formerly an industrial area, River West is home to many artists attracted to the large loft spaces, close proximity to downtown, easy public transportation and great night life. Those lofts not taken by artists, however, befell the fate of similar properties in other neighborhoods: developers gobbled them up for new condominium residences or luxury town homes. As a result, this former center of blue-collar industrial enterprise has risen from the depths of working-class sweat to become one of the trendiest, most sought-after neighborhoods in the city.

THEATRES	Chicago Dramatists. Also, the Chicago Academy for Performing Arts has been in the neighborhood for 25 years.
RENTS	Studio: $950
	One Bed: $1000–$1950
	Two Bed: $1325–$2300
CRIME STATS	Violent Crime: C
	Total Crime: C

Rogers Park

This northernmost neighborhood is popular among actors and artists for so many reasons: it's close to the lake, public transportation is readily available and the rents are still low. Loyola University sits on the eastern edge of the community and is surrounded by the standard collegiate fare—coffee shops, bookstores, restaurants, etc. This is an area where the neighborhood changes from block to block and safety varies, especially at night. Be sure to walk or visit the area during both day and night to test levels of comfort.

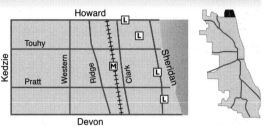

THEATRES	Lifeline, Heartland Studio Theater, The Side Project Theatre
RENTS	Studio: $450–$695 One Bed: $550–$1100 Two Bed: $750–$1900
AVERAGE HOUSING PURCHASE PRICE	$272,313
CRIME STATS	Violent Crime: C Total Crime: B

Coming to Chicago

Roscoe Village

This funky little community situated directly west of Lakeview might soon make Chicago's most endangered neighborhood list. Rent is on the rise—but still reasonable—as Lincoln Parkers continue to spread north and west. Roscoe Village maintains a mellow cafe atmosphere that is rich with bars, restaurants and small shops. It also houses one of Chicago's oldest antique districts.

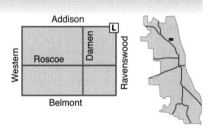

ACTOR BARS	Four Moon Tavern, The Hungry Brain
THEATRES	The Viaduct (just south of the area)
RENTS	Studios: $615 One Bed: $875–$1250 Two Bed: $895–$1800
AVERAGE HOUSING PURCHASE PRICE	$493,929
CRIME STATS	Violent Crime: A Total Crime: B

St. Ben's

Similar in feel to Roscoe Village, St. Ben's is named for the Catholic parish of the area, Saint Benedict's. This neighborhood is primarily residential, with a lot of single-family homes and some apartment buildings. Due to this neighborhood design, parking is decent. Rents are going up, but there are lots of things to do along Lincoln Avenue.

THEATRES	Chicago Comedy Company
RENTS	One Bed: $850–$1050 Two Bed: $1050–$2400
CRIME STATS	Violent Crime: A Total Crime: B

Skokie

Skokie is home to one of the largest Jewish populations in the area. The suburb is diverse, however, containing large communities of Asians and Latinos as well. Skokie is a great option for actors and artists with families; the schools are good, and the area is close to the city. Skokie even has an 'L' extension train called the "Skokie Swift," or the Yellow Line, making public transportation into the city readily available.

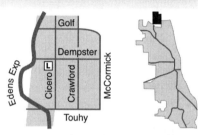

THEATRES	Northlight Theatre, which is housed in the Northshore Center for the Performing Arts
RENTS	One Bed: $650–$800 Two Bed: $975–$1350
AVERAGE HOUSING PURCHASE PRICE	$235,300

Ukrainian Village

Contrary to its name, Ukrainian Village is really quite diverse, housing large communities of Latinos, Italians and, of course, Ukrainians. It's a cultural hotbed that makes the environment ripe for creative endeavor. While public transportation is available only by bus, parking isn't too bad in spots. The rents are reasonable, but it is yet another neighborhood feeling the pangs of gentrification. One distinctive Ukrainian Village trait is a real obligation between neighbors to look out for each other. There are many longtime residents who seem to know everything about everybody. This vigilance can be a relief or a hassle, depending on your point of view.

RENTS	One Bed: $975 Two Bed: $775–$2500
AVERAGE HOUSING PURCHASE PRICE	$441,439
CRIME STATS	Violent Crime: B Total Crime: B

Uptown

Over the past year, the Uptown area has entered a phase of incredible revitalization. This historic neighborhood was in its heyday in the 1920s, then a bustling center of commerce and culture. The heart of this vitality was located at the corner of Lawrence and Broadway, which attracted entertainment seekers and big shots like Al Capone and Charlie Chaplin. Over the years, however, the neighborhood fell victim to disrepair and neglect and became known by the locals as "skid row," with its many homeless and vagrants taking up residence in the low-rent area. But local community groups formed to resurrect the neighborhood, making gentrification an issue. The Uptown Theatre is scheduled for a complete renovation, and developers have become interested in the inexpensive real estate.

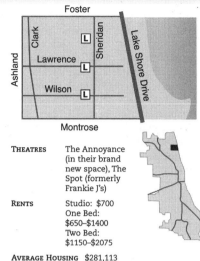

THEATRES	The Annoyance (in their brand new space), The Spot (formerly Frankie J's)
RENTS	Studio: $700 One Bed: $650–$1400 Two Bed: $1150–$2075
AVERAGE HOUSING PURCHASE PRICE	$281,113
CRIME STATS	Violent Crime: B Total Crime: B

West Loop/Greektown

Just west of the Loop is a neighborhood with lots to offer any resident. True to its name, Greektown offers loads of Greek cuisine and culture. There are shops and clubs emphasizing the roots of this rich heritage. Very accessible by both public transportation and car, this former meat market area has been transformed into expensive real estate, with new developments and rehabbed condos popping up everywhere. Harpo Studios and Lou Conte Dance Studio are housed here.

RENTS	Studio: $986–$1205 1 Bedroom: $1075–$1700 2 Bedroom: $1250–$3850
AVERAGE HOUSING PURCHASE PRICE	$335,647
CRIME STATS	Violent Crime: C Total Crime: B

Wicker Park

While gentrification needles at this neighborhood, the residents of Wicker Park try to buck it at every turn. Young, hip and trendy—individuality is golden here. The park itself is just north of the intersection of Damen, North and Milwaukee—the heart of the Wicker Park neighborhood and a hotbed for late-night activity. Public transportation is readily available, and a great help with troublesome parking. Safety has improved significantly over the last few years.

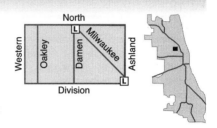

THEATRES	Chopin Theatre, Gorilla Tango Theatre
RENTS	Studio: $825 One Bed: $800–$1200 Two Bed: $1100–$2700
AVERAGE HOUSING PURCHASE PRICE	$443,238
CRIME STATS	Violent Crime: B Total Crime: B

Wrigleyville

Aptly named, Wrigleyville—a neighborhood within the larger Lakeview community—lies directly around the ballpark. While strolling through the neighborhood, there can be no doubt where you are, as you are constantly bombarded with Cubs memorabilia. Great eats and watering holes abound—although most cater to the sports/frat crowd. Living by the ballpark provides endless social opportunities, but the very thing that makes the neighborhood, breaks it too. Parking is terrible. Streets are crowded, and rents are going up. Public transportation, however, is excellent.

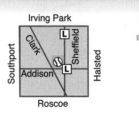

THEATRES	IO (formerly ImprovOlympic), Live Bait Theatre
RENTS	Studios: $650–$935 One Bed: $825–$1200 Two Bed: $1100–$2700
CRIME STATS	Violent Crime: B- Total Crime: B

Temp Agencies

A Personnel Commitment
208 S. LaSalle St., Suite 189
Chicago, IL 60604
888/GET-A-JOB
> See our ad on the
> inside front cover.

Active Temporary Services
3145 N. Lincoln Ave.
Chicago, IL 60657
312/726-5771
www.activetemp.com

Advanced Resources
225 W. Washington St., Suite 500
Chicago, IL 60606
312/422-9333
www.advancedresources.com
kmarzano@advancedresources.com
> For 19 years, ADVANCED RESOURCES LLC
> has provided talented employees with
> access to rewarding TEMPORARY, TEMP-
> TO-HIRE and DIRECT HIRE positions
> at Chicagoland's best companies.
> Advanced specializes in office support,
> and Accounting/Finance. To learn more
> about Advanced Resources LLC, view our
> open positions or to apply on-line, visit
> us at www.advancedresources.com.
> **See our ad on page 24.**

BPS Staffing
200 N. LaSalle St., Suite 1900
Chicago, IL 60601
312/920-6710
www.bpsstaffing.com
bps@bpsstaffing.com

Kelly Services
20 N. Martingale Rd., Suite 140
Schaumburg, IL 60173
847/995-9350
www.kellyservices.com
2423@kellyservices.com

Pro Staff Personnel Services
230 W. Monroe St., Suite 510
Chicago, IL 60606
312/575-2120
www.prostaff.com
chicago.jobs@prostaff@com

Proven Performers
225 W. Washington St.
Chicago, IL 60606
312/917-1111
www.provensolutions.biz
renee.t@provensolutions.biz

Right Employment Center
55 W. Monroe St.
Chicago, IL 60603
312/427-3136
www.stivers.com

Select Staffing
208 S. LaSalle St., Suite 688
Chicago, IL 60604
312/849-2229
www.select-staffing.com
wallen@select-staffing.com

Seville Staffing
180 N. Michigan Ave., Suite 1510
Chicago, IL 60601
312/368-1272
www.sevillestaffing.com
mail@sevillestaffing.com
> Seville Staffing has been providing
> Chicago-area talent with temporary
> Office Support jobs such as:
> Administrative Assistant, Word
> Processor, Reception, Data Entry
> and Customer Service Clerk positions
> since 1979. We also offer weekly pay,
> vacation pay, health insurance, and
> respect for the work you do. Call
> 312/368-1272 for an appointment.
> **See our ad on the back cover.**

Smart Staffing
29 S. LaSalle St., Suite 635
Chicago, IL 60603
312/696-5306
www.smartstaffing.com

Spherion
10 S. Riverside Plz., Suite 2200
Chicago, IL 60606
312/781-7220
www.spherion.com

Staffing The City
211 W. Wacker Dr., Suite 700
Chicago, IL 60606
312/346-3400
www.staffingthecity.com
info@staffingthecity.com

Temporary Opportunities
53 W. Jackson Blvd., Suite 215
Chicago, IL 60604
312/922-5400
www.opgroup.com

The Larko Group
11 S. LaSalle St., Suite 1720
Chicago, IL 60603
312/857-2300
www.thelarkogroup.com

Unique Office Services
203 N. Wabash Ave., Suite 518
Chicago, IL 60601
312/332-4183
uniqueofcsvc@aol.com

Venturi Staffing Partners
222 N. LaSalle St., Suite 450
Chicago, IL 60601
312/541-4141
www.venturipartners.com
chicago@venturipartners.com

Watson Dwyer Staffing
25 E. Washington St., Suite 1927
Chicago, IL 60602
312/899-8030
www.watsondwyer.com

Wordspeed
200 N. Dearborn St., Suite 807
Chicago, IL 60601
312/201-1171
wordspeed@ameritech.net

Knowing the Lingo—
A Valuable Tool

BY MECHELLE MOE

ach industry has its own vocabulary, and the acting world—on-camera or on-stage—is no exception. Below is a short list of terms you will run across while out in the field.

ACTORS' EQUITY ASSOCIATION Stage actors and stage managers labor union (see *Unions and Organizations*).

AFTRA American Federation of Television and Radio Artists (see *Unions and Organizations*).

BITE AND SMILE A very literal term for a type of commercial that is generally MOS (Mit Out Sound) and advertising food products. Think of that extra fresh stick of gum you've been craving, pop it in your mouth and give a sparkling smile to show how much you enjoy it.

BOOKING A booking means that you've been hired for a job, and usually refers to on-camera work.

BREAKDOWNS A listing given to agents which details production company projects and cast requirements such as type, age range, audition/callback date, shoot date, casting director, etc.

BUYOUT A buyout is a contractual agreement that states a set fee the talent will receive if they agree to opt out of all rights to future money, i.e. residuals.

CALLBACK Basically, you've made the first cut in the audition process and are invited back to the second or final round of auditions.

COLD READING An actor auditions with script in hand—not memorized or partially-memorized—without a lot of prep time.

COMPOSITE/COMP CARD A comp card is a composite of several photographs that exhibit different looks or styles and reflect various aspects of your personality. Generally, this is required if you are being submitted for print or modeling work.

COPY The script for a commercial audition, sometimes only one or two lines long.

CRAFT SERVICE The job of craft service is to feed the cast and crew during a shoot. They provide breakfast, lunch and dinner as well as snacks. Mandatory on a union set, but not always provided for non-union gigs.

DAILIES This refers to the film shot—usually the day before—that is developed and viewed on a daily basis during an ongoing shoot as a means of quality control.

EARPROMPTER This is an earpiece connected to a small tape recorder that actors wear during taping in order to help them navigate long, technical scripts quickly. Industrials or any type of live narration event typically require actors to be earprompter proficient.

EXCLUSIVITY A contractual agreement between an actor and talent agency that prohibits the talent from listing with or soliciting work from other competing agencies. In Chicago, actors tend to be multi-listed with agencies rather than going exclusive.

EXTRA An actor hired to play a minor part or serve as background to a scene. These parts typically have few or no lines. It definitely is grunt work that garners little respect; but if you want to familiarize yourself with the process, this is your opportunity to be a fly on the wall.

HEADSHOT & RESUME A professional 8×10 photo of yourself with your resume attached to the back. The resume lists previous work experience on-camera or on-stage, along with any training or special skills.

ICED Slang used to refer to talent who have been put on hold for a project—there is potential for booking, but also a high chance of cancellation.

INDUSTRIAL Training and educational films made for corporations.

LIVE INDUSTRIAL Live performances about products or services held for corporations.

LOOKSEE It's just what it sounds like—you are invited down so casting directors and clients can take a quick look to see if you're the type they're looking for.

MONOLOGUE A memorized selection of text (usually from a play) performed at an audition. Auditors will generally set requirements for length (one to three minutes is pretty normal) and type (i.e., classical or contemporary).

MOS Mit Out Sound are moments on screen where there is no dialogue, but there are reaction shots or visuals.

MUST JOIN You're considered to have must join status if you book a SAG union job after 30 days from which you booked your first union job. However, you do not have to join the union if you do not book another union job after this time period.

ON-CAMERA Refers to anything on-camera such as TV, film, commercials and industrials.

ON HOLD The casting director will put an actor on hold if the client wants them for a job but has not formally hired them yet. The actor may not book any other jobs during this period which conflict with the first job's production dates.

OPEN CALL/"CATTLE CALL" A mass audition held to find new or inexperienced talent. This usually means dealing with hundreds of people, long lines and long waiting periods on the chance of being discovered.

PILOT A mock-up of a new television show producers try to sell to the networks; if the show is "picked up," it usually receives a trial run of 13 episodes.

PILOT SEASON Production companies start casting next season's shows during late winter to early spring. Breakdowns are distributed nationwide, but casting preference is given to Los Angeles actors.

PRINT WORK Print photography—open to both actors and models—used in the advertisement of a product. Think magazines, billboards or the product container itself.

REEL Usually three to five minutes in length, the reel is comprised of brief clips highlighting your best work on-camera, and can also include stage video. Investing in a good reel is not essential for working in Chicago, but it is a required marketing tool for LA and New York.

RESIDUALS A payment made to the talent for each additional showing of a recorded television show, commercial, print job, voice-over, etc.

SAG Screen Actors Guild (see *Unions and Organizations*).

SIDES Usually one to two pages of the script made available to the actor for the audition. Memorization isn't generally required, but you should be extremely familiar and comfortable with the text.

SLATE At the top of an on-camera audition, casting directors will ask you to "slate." This is the term used for stating your name and, often, your agency to the camera before you begin your audition piece.

STAND-IN An individual who matches certain characteristics (height, weight, skin tone) of the talent and stands in position while the crew is lighting the scene and setting up for the shot.

TAFT-HARTLEY Also known as the National Labor Relations Act, Taft-Hartley is a term used by unions to define a potential new member's status. The act allows non-union talent to work one or more union jobs within a 30-day time period of the first booking without having to join the union. Talent must join after that period in order to book any future union job.

TEAR SHEET A hard copy example of print work that has been ripped out of a magazine or product's package.

TELEPROMPTER A monitor set at camera level that displays the script for the actor to read.

TYPE A generic classification that actors are broken down into in terms of their look and personality. To figure out your type, ask yourself: What's my realistic age range? Am I more like the kid just out of college, or the young mom or dad? What ethnic types do I pass for? What's my level of education? Annual income? Sense of humor—loud and gregarious or sarcastic and dry, etc. Also look at the basic stereotypes offered on television and see which way you lean or who you most look like.

VOICE-OVER The voice of an unseen actor in TV, film and radio spots, etc. Voice-over work can be anything from a radio commercial to a book-on-tape to your favorite cartoon character.

2 The Actor's Tools

Accountants & Tax Preparers

Bob Behr
4738 N. LaPorte Ave.
Chicago, IL 60630
773/685-7721
bobster@ameritech.net

David Turrentine, E. A.
Income Tax Service
2610 W. Eastwood Ave.
Chicago, IL 60625
773/509-1798
www.davidturrentine.com
david@davidturrentine.com

H. Gregory Mermel
2835 N. Sheffield Ave., Ste. 311
Chicago, IL 60657
773/525-1778
greg@gregmermel.com

H&R Block
179 W. Washington St.
Chicago, IL 60602
312/424-0268
www.hrblock.com

Joel N. Goldblatt, Ltd.
515 N. State St., Ste. 2200
Chicago, IL 60610
312/372-9322

Weiner & Lahn, PC
930 W. 175th St., Ste3-SE-B
Homewood, IL 60430
708/799-0123

Answering Services

Burke Communications
P.O. Box 4152
Oak Park, IL 60303
708/383-8580
www.burketelecom.com
tburke@burketelecom.com

Attorneys

Chicago Bar Association
Lawyer Referral
321 S. Plymouth Ct.
Chicago, IL 60604
312/554-2000
www.chicagobar.org

Chicago Volunteer Legal Services
100 N. LaSalle St., Ste. 900
Chicago, IL 60602
312/332-1624
www.cvls.org

Dale M. Golden
25 E. Washington St., Ste. 1400
Chicago, IL 60602
312/201-9730
www.dalegoldenlaw.com

Jay B. Ross & Associates, PC
840 W. Grand Ave.
Chicago, IL 60622
312/633-9000
www.jaybr.com
music_law@msn.com

Joel N. Goldblatt, Ltd.
515 N. State St., Ste. 2200
Chicago, IL 60610
312/372-9322

Lawyers for the Creative Arts
William E. Rather, Executive Director
213 W. Institute Pl., Ste. 401
Chicago, IL 60610
312/649-4111
wrather@law-arts.org

Robert Labate, Holland Knight, LLC
131 S. Dearborn St., 30th Flr.
Chicago, IL 60603
312/263-3600
www.hklaw.com

Timothy S. Kelly
55 E. Washington St., Ste. 1441
Chicago, IL 60602
312/641-3560

Tom Fezzey
600 W. Roosevelt Rd., Ste. B1
Wheaton, IL 60187
630/909-0909
www.fezzey.com

William Borah and Associates
39 S. LaSalle St., Ste. 915
Chicago, IL 60611
708/799-0066
borahlaw@sbcglobal.net

Dance Supplies

Big 'N' Little Shoes
3142 W. 111th St.
Chicago, IL 60655
773/239-6066
www.bignlittleshoes.com

Chicago Dance Supply
Leni Hoppenworth
5301 N. Clark St.
Chicago, IL 60640
773/728-5344
chicagodancesupply.com
questions@chicagodancesupply.com

Illinois Theatrical
P.O. Box 34284
Chicago, IL 60634
800/745-3777
www.illinoistheatrical.com
esupport@illinoistheatrical.com

Leo's Dancewear Inc.
1900 N. Narragansett Ave.
Chicago, IL 60639
773/889-7700
www.leosdancewear.com
info@leosdancewear.com

Motion Unlimited
218 S. Wabash Ave., 8th Flr.
Chicago, IL 60604
312/922-3330
www.motionunlimiteddancewear.com
motionunlimited@motionunlimited-dancewear.com

Serena's Cirlce
773/459-4802
www.serenascircle.com
admin@serenascircle.com

Demo Tapes & CDs

See Chapter 5, "On-Camera and Voice-Over," on page 115.

Ear Prompters

Credible Communication, Inc.
155 Little John Tr. NE
Atlanta, GA 30309
404/892-0660
www.ear-prompter.com

Insurance

Myers-Briggs and Company, Inc.
300 S. Wacker Dr., Ste. 2000
Chicago, IL 60606
312/263-3215
www.myersbriggs.com

Paczolt Financial Group
913 W. Hillgrove Ave.
LaGrange, IL 60525
708/579-3128
www.paczolt.com

Ronald Shapero Insurance Associates
260 E. Chestnut St., Ste. 3406
Chicago, IL 60611
312/337-7133
www.lowcosthighbenefitinsurance.com

2 The Actor's Tools

Teeth whitening – Free!

After your photographer gives you the digital file
or your print, the photo reprint process begins –
for headshots, comp cards, postcards,
litho prints, or business cards.

Our last minute "touch-ups" are appreciated by actors,
models and even photographers. And we'll show you
an actual print before running your reprints.
We want you to have a bright smile!

Stop in, or email us: jbaldwin@a-bphoto.com

Open Saturdays 9:30 - 12:30 (Sept.-May)

A & B
Photo & Print

650 W. Lake St. • #220 • Chicago 60661

(312) 454-4554

Prices? Check us out: www.a-bphoto.com

Makeup Artists

Darcy McGrath
312/337-1353
Sandy Morris
773/549-4951
www.sandyfaceartist.com
Che Sguardo Makeup Studio
161 W. Illinois St.
Chicago, IL 60610
312/527-0821
Marianne Strokirk Salon
361 W. Chestnut St.
Chicago, IL 60610
312/944-4428
www.mariannestrokirk.com
info@mariannestrokirk.com

Marilyn Miglin Institute
Marilyn Miglin
112 E. Oak St.
Chicago, IL 60611
312/266-4600
www.marilyn-miglin.com
Media Hair & Makeup Group
708/848-8400
Transformations by Rori
110 S. Arlington Heights Rd.
Arlington Heights, IL 60301
847/454-0600
www.transformationsbyrori.com
transformme2@transformationsbyrori.com

Photo Reproductions

A&B Photograhy
650 W. Lake St., 2nd Flr.
Chicago, IL 60661
312/454-4554
www.a-bphoto.com
jbaldwin@a-bphoto.com
See our ad on page 34.
ABC Pitcures
Carrie Mitchell
1867 E. Florida St.
Springfield, MO 65803
417/869-3456
www.abcpictures.com
contactus@abcpictures.com
See our ad on page 35.
National GraphX
9240 W.Belmont Ave.
Franklin Park, IL 60131
847/671-1122
www.nationalphoto.com
See our ad on page 41.

New Graf Foto
222 Merchandise Mart Plaza
Room 214
Chicago, IL 60654
312/254-5343
Great Graphics Photoscan
646 Bryn Mawr St.
Orlando, FL 32804
800/352-6367
www.ggphotoscan.com
greg@ggphotoscan.com
Quantity Photo
119 W. Hubbard St., 2nd Flr.
Chicago, IL 60610
312/644-8288
www.quantityphoto.com
sales@quantityphoto.com

Photographers

Brad Baskin
850 N. Milwaukee Ave.
Chicago, IL 60622
312/733-2192
www.bradbaskin.com
photos@bradbaskin.com

Nancy P. Stanley
773/871-1396

Aaron Gang Photography
1016 N. Ashland Ave.
Chicago, IL 60622
773/782-4363
www.aarongang.com
info@aarongang.com
    See our ad on page 36.

Allan Murray
1717 N. Hudson Ave.
Chicago, IL 60614
312/337-0286
almurray7@aol.com

Art Ketchum Studios
2215 S. Michigan Ave.
Chicago, IL 60616
312/842-1406
www.artketchum.com

Audrey Keller Photography
1702 W. Carmen, Suite 2W
Chicago, IL 60640
773/8-STUDIO(878-8346)
www.akphotodesign.com
audrey@akphotodesign.com

Have confidence in Audrey Keller Photography. Being comfortable with your photographer is important to insure your personality will shine in your photos. Please call for a FREE consultation. You will meet Audrey and discuss your personal needs ensuring the photo session is tailored to your specific requirements. Credit cards accepted.

Bauwerks Progressive Photography
2475 N. Clybourn
Chicago, IL 60614
773/529-4199
www.bauwerks.com
contact@bauwerks.com

Brian McConkey
312 N. May St., Suite 6J
Chicago, IL 60607
312/563-1357
www.brianmcconkeyphotography.com
brian@brianmcconkeyphotography.com
    See our ad on page 38.

Bryan Swisher Photography
312/643-1138
www.bryanswisher.com

Camera 1
3946 N. Monticello Ave.
Chicago, IL 60618
773/539-1119
www.camera1chicago.com
camera1joe@yahoo.com

Cat Conrad Photography
510 W. Belmont Ave., Suite 1810
Chicago, IL 60657
773/459-3571
www.catconradphoto.com
catconrad@sbcglobal.net
    See our ad on page 36.

Classic Photography, Inc.
John Karl Breun
The Tower Center
200 E. Evergreen Ave., Suite 128
Mount Prospect, IL 60056
847/259-8373
www.classicphoto.com
jkb@classicphoto.com

Costume Images
3634 W. Fullerton Ave.
Chicago, IL 60647
773/276-8971
www.costumeimagesphotography.net
costumeimages@comcast.net

Dale Fahey
773/973-5757
ddale2@rcn.com

Dan Duverney
1937 W. Division St., 1st Flr.
Chicago, IL 60622
773/252-6639
www.duverneyphoto.com
daniel@DuVerneyPhoto.com

Daniel Byrnes Photography
1544 N. Wieland St.
Studio B
Chicago, IL 60610
312/337-1174
www.danielbyrnesstudios.com
dbyrnes@danielbyrnesstudios.com

David Zak Photography
1450 W. Webster Ave., East Entrance
Chicago, IL 60614
773/612-1229
www.davidgzak.com
davidzak@gmail.com

DDT Photo
Donte Tatum
1819 S. Carpenter St.
Chicago, IL 60608
312/563-0396
ddtphoto@sbcglobal.net

Deone Jahnke
228 S. 1st
Milwaukee, WI 53204
414/224-8360
www.deonejahnke.com
deone@deonejahnke.com

Edda Taylor Photographie
Courthouse Square, Suite 304
Crown Point, IN 46307
219/662-1972
www.eddataylor.com
eddataylor@sbcglobal.net

Elan Photography
1944 University Ln.
Lisle, IL 60532
630/969-1972
www.elanphotography.com

G. Thomas Ward Photography
5010 N. Wolcott Ave.
Chicago, IL 60640
773/271-6813
www.thepeoplephotographer.com
gtwinchgo@aol.com

*G. Thomas Ward Photography has been
the choice for Chicago performers since
1992. Please check out my work at
www.thepeoplephotographer.com and
judge for yourself. Agents constantly
comment on my clean style and honest
approach, and the way the performer's
personality shines through. You won't
be disappointed. Thanks!*

Gary Trantafil
3927 N. Spaulding Ave.
Chicago, IL 60618
312/666-1029
www.trantafilphotography.com

Gerber/Scarpelli Photography
110 N. Peoria St.
Chicago, IL 60607
312/455-1144
www.gerberscarpelli.com
mike@gerberscarpelli.com

IronHorse Productions
3310 S. Aberdeen St., Suite 1-A
Chicago, IL 60608
773/890-4355

James Banasiak Photography
400 N. Racine Ave., #217
Chicago, IL 60622
646/234-0130
www.jbheadshots.com
james@jbheadshots.com

Jean Whiteside
2041 Arrowhead Ct.
Geneva, IL 60134
630/845-2611
www.jeanwhitesidephoto.com
whitesidephoto@yahoo.com

Jennifer Girard Photography
1455 W. Roscoe St.
Chicago, IL 60657
773/871-7762
www.jennifergirard.com
jengirard3@comcast.net

*A head shot doesn't have to be beauti-
ful, it has to be true, then it's beautiful!*
JENNIFER GIRARD *former model/actress,
head shot photographer for 30 years.
You'll receive proofs immediately after
the session. I will shoot until you love
your pictures. Splitting a session is
accepted. www.jennifergirard.com.
773/871-7762 jengirard3@comcast.net*
See our ad on page 42.

Borter Wagner Photography
711 N. Milwaukee Ave.
Chicago, IL 60607
312/339-3909
www.borterwagner.com
perform@borterwagner.com

John Abbott
4015 N. Whipple St.
Chicago, IL 60618
773/583-3823
www.johnabbott.net
john@johnabbott.net
See our ad on page 38.

Johnny Knight Photo
5315 N. Clark St. #266
Chicago, IL 60640
773/368-8707
www.johnnyknightphoto.com
johnny@johnnyknightphoto.com

*I try to make the headshot experience
comfortable, relaxed, and fun. Bring
music, bring a friend, kick back and
have fun on-camera. Also, I like experi-
menting with headshot style, so if you
want a shot that's unique, I'd love to
customize a shot for you.*

Joseph Amenta Photography
555 W. Madison St., Suite 3802
Chicago, IL 60661
773/248-2488

Keith Claunch
5049 N. Avers Ave.
Chicago, IL 60625
312/285-6074
www.keithclaunch.com
kc@keithclaunch.com

Kenneth Simmons
3026 E. 80th St.
Chicago, IL 60617
773/721-7393
ksimmonschicago@hotmail.com

Larry Lapidus Photography
2650 W. Belden Ave., #304
Chicago, IL 60647
773/235-3333
www.lapidusphoto.com
larry@lapidusphoto.com

Michael Brosilow Photography
1370 N. Milwaukee Ave.
Chicago, IL 60622
773/235-4696
www.brosilow.com
mb@brosilow.com

Michael J. Kardas Photography
2635 N. Albany Ave.
Chicago, IL 60647
773/227-7925
kardas@kardasphotography.com

Mike Canale Photography
614 Davis St.
Evanston, IL 60201
847/864-0146
www.mikecanalephoto.com

*$60 off current session price with this
ad! Performing arts photographer with
extensive experience providing best quality color and b&w headshots. Just minutes away, conveniently located in the
Giordano Dance Center, 614 Davis Street,
Evanston (one block from CTA & Metra
train stops). Visit www.mikecanale-
photo.com for more info & portfolio.*

Don't Panic
Get Shot Right

Color and B&W Actor Headshots
Color Comps
Location & Studio Shoots
Promotional Podcasts & Quicktime videos
Actor & Theatre website hosting and design
Press Kits & PR shoots for Theatre

Online print ordering via private web gallery
Credit Cards Accepted

REP3 is more than "just another photographer"
he is an artist with a camera and fellow Thespian.
Potter is an Ensemble member and founder of the
Piccolo Theatre, he knows what you need & has
the talent to produce it.

Joyce Sloane, producer of The Second City says,
"I recommend Rob highly; his photographs, input
and suggestions result in excellent, professional
marketing devises for the Actor."

312.226.2060   **www.REP3.com**

Robert Erving Potter III

REP3

www.REP3.com
312-226-2060
Potter@REP3.com

Artist / Photographer

Piccolo Theatre Founder

Talent: Kimberly Sorenson

p+g photography
Paul Grigonis
773/505-3047
paul@pplusgdesign.com
www.pplusgdesign.com

Papadakis Photography
17 Lexington Rd.
Barrington, IL 60010
847/428-4400
www.papadakisphotography.com

Pete Stenberg Photography
400 N. Wells St., Suite 400
Chicago, IL 60610
312/718-3363
web.mac.com/pdsphoto1
pdsphoto1@mac.com

Peter Bosy Photography, Inc.
6435 Indian Head Tr.
Indian Head Park, IL 60525
708/246-3778
www.peterbosy.com/faces.html
peterbosy@aol.com

Pret-a-Poser Photography
Mark Sojdehee
3656 N. Lincoln Ave., Suite G
Chicago, IL 60613
773/248-2211
www.pretaposer.com
msojdehee@sbcglobal.net

Rance Rizzutto Photography
720 W. Waveland Ave., #GRDN
Chicago, IL 60613
773/387-0475
www.rancerizzutto.com
photo@rancerizzutto.com
> *Your headshot should open doors
> and give agents a realistic impression
> of who you are, personality and all.
> At Rance Rizzutto Photography we
> strive to capture the real you in the
> best light possible.*

Rascon Design Photography
Otto Rascon
3347 W. Warren Blvd.
Chicago, IL 60624
773/430-4785
www.photo.rascondesign.com
otto@photo.rascondesign.com

REP3.com
aka Robert Erving Potter III
312/226-2060
www.rep3.com
potter@rep3.com
See our ad on page 40.

Rick Mitchell, Inc
652 W. Grand Ave.
Chicago, IL 60610
312/829-1700
www.rickmitchellphoto.com
rmitchell@aol.com

Rubinic Photography
319 N. Western Ave.
Chicago, IL 60612
312/733-8901
www.rubinic.com
info@rubinic.com

Sandra Bever
1200 Wilcox St.
Joliet, IL 60435
815/723-3051
www.sandrabever.com
sandrabever@comcast.net

Sara Levinson
1142 S. Michigan Ave.
Chicago, IL 60607
312/583-0338
www.saralevinsonphoto.com
sara@saralevinsonphoto.com

Sharleen Acciari
1007 W. Webster Ave.
Chicago, IL 60614
773/248-1273
cujosharleen60614@yahoo.com

Starbelly Studios
Timmy Samuels
5215 N. Ravenswood Ave., Suite 203
Chicago, IL 60640
773/551-0018
www.starbellystudios.com

Steve Greiner Photography
1437 W. Thomas St.
Chicago, IL 60622
773/227-4375
www.stevegreiner.com
steve@stevegreiner.com
> *We are conveniently located near the Division stop on the Blue Line and right off the Kennedy expressway. Our emphasis is on your satisfaction and making you comfortable. We take the time to create personalized headshots that will totally thrill you. Please call for a free consultation.*

Suzanne Plunkett Photographs
3047 N. Lincoln Ave., Suite 300
Chicago, IL 60657
773/477-3775
www.suzanneplunkettphotographs.com
suzplunk@comcast.com

Taylor Fashion and Commercial Photography
1143 E. 81st St.
Chicago, IL 60619
773/978-1505

The Look Photography
Randy Stueve
6204 Roger Ln.
Hodgkins, IL 60525
708/352-0164
thelookphotography@hotmail.com

Wayne Cable Photography
312 N. Carpenter St.
Chicago, IL 60607
312/226-0303
www.waynecable.com
infor@waynecable.com

Yamashiro Studio
2034 W. Grand Ave.
Chicago, IL 60612
773/883-0440
www.yamashirostudio.com

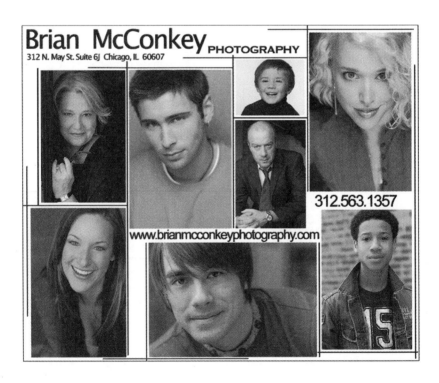

Reels

See Chapter 5, "On-Camera and Voice-Over," on page 115.

Resumes

Bob Behr
4738 N. LaPorte Ave.
Chicago, IL 60630
773/685-7721
bobster@ameritech.net

Ink Well
112 W. Illinois St.
Chicago, IL 60610
312/644-4700
www.inkwellchicago.com
graphics@inkwellchicago.com

Sheet Music

8 Notes
www.8notes.com
Beautiful Music
www.beautifulmusicdg.com
Carl Fischer Music
65 Bleecker St.
New York, NY 10012
212/777-0900
www.carlfischer.com
cf-info@carlfischer.com
Free Sheet Music
www.freesheetmusic.net

JW Pepper of Chicago
130 E. St. Charles Rd., Suite A
Carol Stream, IL 60197
630/462-0787
www.jwpepper.com
Music Go Round
1658 N. Milwaukee Ave.
Chicago, IL 60647
773/342-2460
www.musicgoround.com
Music Notes
www.musicnotes.com
Sheet Music Direct
www.sheetmusicdirect.us
Sheet Music Plus
www.sheetmusicplus.com

Trade Papers

Act One Reports
640 N. LaSalle St., Suite 535
Chicago, IL 60610
312/787-9384
www.actone.com
> *Updating listings of agencies, casting directors, photographers, and industry-related information.*

American Theatre Magazine
520 8th Ave., 24th floor
New York, NY 10018-4156
212/609-5900
www.tcg.org
at@tcg.org
Audition News
P.O. Box 250
Bloomingdale, IL 60108
630/272-5510

Backstage
770 Broadway, 6th Flr.
New York, NY 10003
646/654-5700
www.backstage.com
Backstage West
5055 Wilshire Blvd., 5th Flr.
Los Angeles, CA 90036
323/525-2354
www.backstage.com
bsweditorial@backstage.com
Breakdown Services, Ltd.
2140 Cotner Ave.
Los Angeles, CA 90025
310/276-9166
www.breakdownservices.com

Callboard
> 870 Market St., Suite 375
> San Francisco, CA 94102
> 415/430-1140
> *www.theatrebayarea.org*

Chicago Creative Directory
> 333 N. Michigan Ave., Suite 810
> Chicago, IL 60610
> 312/236-7337
> *www.creativedir.com*
> info@creativedir.com

Equity News
> 165 W. 46th St.
> New York, NY 10036
> 212/719-9570

Hollywood Reporter
> 5055 Wilshire Blvd.
> Los Angeles, CA 90036
> 323/525-2150
> *www.hollywoodreporter.com*

PerformInk
> P.O.Box 459
> Flossmoor, IL 60422
> 708/647-8100
> *www.perfomink.com*
>> *The Chicago Area's most comprehensive*
>> *source for audition notices, training*
>> *informatin, and Chicago theatre and*
>> *film information.*

Reel Chicago
> Ruth L. Ratny
> *www.reelchicago.org*

Ross Reports Television and Film
> Bruce B. Morris, Editor in Chief
> 770 Broadway, 4th Floor
> New York, NY 10003
> 646/654-5730
> *www.rossreports.com*

Screen Magazine
> 16 W. Erie St.
> Chicago, IL 60610
> 312/664-5236
> *www.screenmag.com*

Theatre Directories
> P.O. Box 159
> Dorset, VT 5251
> 802/867-9333
> *www.theatredirectories.com*

Variety
> *www.variety.com*

Key of Symbols Used in This Chapter

A Red Orchid Theatre

E Sc D CAT I

1531 North Wells Street
Chicago, IL 60610
312/943-8722
arot@a-red-orchid.com
www.aredorchidtheatre.org
Artistic Director
Guy Van Swearingen
Managing Director
Thomas Murray
Nearest El
Sedgwick (Brown); Clark/Division
(Red)
Send Headshots to
Guy Van Swearingen

Ensemble-Based
This company has a core group of actors who may get preferential consideration in casting.

Accepts Scripts
Are you a playwright? This company welcomes new, unproduced plays.

Accepts Synopses
Some companies would prefer to read a short summary of your script.

Accepts Director's Proposals
Are you a director? This company will consider your idea for a show.

Equity Contract
Don't worry – we'll define these terms in Chapter 6, "Unions and Organizations."

Theatres - Equity

A Red Orchid Theatre

E **ESc** **RD** CAT I

1531 N. Wells St.
Chicago, IL 60610
312/943-8722
arot@aredorchid.com
www.aredorchidtheatre.org
Artistic Director
Guy Van Swearingen
Managing Director
Thomas Murray
Nearest Public Transit
Sedgwick (Brown Line);
Clark/Division (Red Line)
Send Headshots to
Guy Van Swearingen

> With impeccable acting, A Red Orchid
> has garnered a reputation for producing
> intensely intimate shows that reflect the
> fragile beauty of life on the edge.
> Founded in 1993.

About Face Theatre

ESy CAT VI

1222 W. Wilson Ave., 2nd Floor West
Chicago, IL 60640
773/784-8565
mailbox@aboutfacetheatre.com
www.aboutfacetheatre.com
Artistic Director
Eric Rosen
Executive Director
Greg Copeland
Budget
$1.1 million
Send Headshots to
Heather Chappell, Production &
Artistic Coordinator

> About Face Theatre creates exceptional,
> innovative and adventurous plays to
> advance the national dialogue on
> gender and sexual identity. Starting
> non-Equity pay varies.

American Players Theatre

E Special Agreement

P.O. Box 819
Spring Green, WI 53588
608/588-7401
608/588-2361 - Box Office
www.playinthewoods.org
Artistic Director
David Frank
Budget
$4.5 million
Send Headshots to
Brenda DeVita, Casting Director

> APT is a professional, Equity, classical,
> outdoor theatre located on wooded 110
> acres. The theatre annually produces five
> plays in rotating repertory. Shakespeare
> is the heart of APT's work, supplemented
> by other classics in the Western Canon.
> Starting non-Equity pay is $325 plus
> housing. Founded in 1979.

American Theater Company

E **ESy** CAT II

1909 W. Byron St.
Chicago, IL 60613
773/929-5009
773/929-1031 - Box Office
info@atcweb.org
www.atcweb.org
Artistic Director
Damon Kiely
Budget
$500,000
Nearest Public Transit
Irving Park (Brown Line)
Send Headshots to
Adam Silver, Casting Director

> American Theater Company is an
> ensemble of artists committed to pro-
> ducing new and classic American sto-
> ries that ask the question, "What does
> it mean to be an American?" Founded
> in 1985.

Annoyance Theatre
🏛E 🖹D Letter of Agreement

4840 N Broadway
Chicago, IL 60640
773/561-4664
773/561-4665 - Box Office
mike@annoyanceproductions.com
www.theannoyance.com
Artistic Director
Mick Napier
Managing Director
Mike Canale
Executive Director
Jennifer Estlin
Nearest Public Transit
Lawrence (Red Line)
Send Headshots to
Mike Canale

> Annoyance develops original musicals
> and plays through improvisation. They
> also feature improvisational shows.
> Starting non-Equity pay varies.
> Founded in 1988.

Apple Tree Theatre
CAT III

1850 Green Bay Rd., Ste 100
Highland Park, IL 60035
847/432-8223
847/432-4335 - Box Office
ccaplinger@appletreetheatre.com
www.appletreetheatre.com
Executive Artistic Director
Eileen Boevers
Budget
Approximately $900,000
Nearest Public Transit
Highland Park
(Metra Union Pacific North)
Send Headshots to
Eileen Boevers

> Apple Tree serves the Northern Suburbs
> with award-winning Equity theatre and
> a first-class acting workshop for kids.
> Founded in 1973.

The Artistic Home
🏛E 🖹Sc 🖹D CAT N

1420 W. Irving Park Rd.
Chicago, IL 60613
773/404-1100
866/811-4111 - Box Office
theartistichome@sbcglobal.net
www.theartistichome.org
Artistic Director
Kathy Scambiatterra
Managing Director
Ed Krystosek
Budget
$130,000
Nearest El
Sheridan (Red Line) or
Irving Park (Brown Line)
Send Headshots to
Kathy Scambiatterra

> In an intimate space, the Artistic Home
> readdresses classics and rarely-pro-
> duced plays that are actor-driven and
> seek to ignite an audience's imagina-
> tion. Starting non-Equity pay is $100
> per show. Founded in 1998.

Black Ensemble Theater
🏛E 🖹Sc 🖹D CAT I

4520 N. Beacon St.
Chicago, IL 60640
773/769-0964
773/769-4451 - Box Office
blackensemble@aol.com
www.blackensembletheater.org
Executive Director
Jackie Taylor
Budget
$1.4 million
Nearest Public Transit
Wilson & Broadway (Red Line)
Send Headshots to
Jackie Taylor

> The Black Ensemble Theater produces
> original musicals based on the African-
> American experience in the United
> States. Starting non-Equity pay is
> $40 per show. Founded in 1976.

Buffalo Theatre Ensemble

E **D** CAT I

McAninch Arts Center
425 Fawell Blvd.
Glen Ellyn, IL 60137
630/942-2137
630/942-4000 - Box Office
www.cod.edu/artscntr
Connie Canaday Howard
Nearest Public Transit
College Ave. (Metra to #706 Pace Bus)
Send Headshots to
Connie Canaday Howard

> *Buffalo Theatre Ensemble (BTE) is rooted in the idea that an acting ensemble and company, who have a history of working together and have developed a sense of trust and community, can create better art. All roles are paid, but non-Equity pay not specified. Founded in 1986.*

Chicago Children's Theatre

TYA

1464 N. Milwaukee Ave., 2nd floor
Chicago, IL 60622
773/227-0180
info@chicagochildrenstheatre.org
www.chicagochildrenstheatre.org
Artistic Director
Jacqueline Russell
Executive Director
Claude Binder
Budget
$3 million
Send Headshots to
Jamie Abelson, Artistic Assistant

> *Chicago Children's Theatre aspires to enrich our community through diverse and significant theatrical programming that engages and inspires the child in all of us. Founded in 2004.*

Chicago Dramatists

CAT I

1105 W. Chicago Ave.
Chicago, IL 60622
312/633-0630
newplays@chicagodramatists.org
www.chicagodramatists.org
Artistic Director
Russ Tutterow
Managing Director
Brian Loevner
Budget
$470,000
Nearest Public Transit
Chicago (Blue Line)
Send Headshots to
Russ Tutterow

> *Since 1979, Chicago Dramatists, the playwrights' theatre, has devoted all of its resources and programming to its singular mission of developing new plays and nurturing playwrights. Starting non-Equity pay is $50 a week.*

Chicago Shakespeare Theater

CAT VI

800 E. Grand Ave.
Chicago, IL 60611
312/595-5656
312/595-5600 - Box Office
www.chicagoshakes.com
Artistic Director
Barbara Gaines
Executive Director
Criss Henderson
Budget
$13 million
Nearest Public Transit
Grand and State (Red Line)
Send Headshots to
Bob Mason, Casting Director

> *The mission of Chicago Shakespeare Theater is to bring to life the plays of William Shakespeare and to present other great performances for audiences from all walks of life and from around the world. Non-Equity pay is competitive with other theatres of its size. Founded in 1986.*

Collaboraction

ⒺSc **⒭D** CAT N

437 N. Wolcott Ave.
Chicago, IL 60622
312/226-9633
info@collaboraction.org
www.collaboraction.org
Executive Artistic Director
Anthony Moseley
Budget
$130,000 (2004)
Send Headshots to
Sarah Gittenstein, Casting

> *Collaboraction is an award winning theatre-based artist collective dedicated to a paradigm of evolving entertainment. Non-Equity pay is $100 stipend per production. Founded in 1997.*

Congo Square Theatre

ⒶⒺ CAT N

2936 N. Southport Ave., Suite 210
Chicago, IL 60660
773/296-1108
312/587-2292 - Box Office
atdouglas125@congosquaretheatre.org
www.congosquaretheatre.org
Artistic Director
Derrick Sanders
Budget
$625,000
Nearest Public Transit
Chicago (Brown and Purple Lines)
Send Headshots to
Aaron Todd Douglas, Associate
Artistic Director

> *Congo Square Theatre is primarily an actor ensemble-driven theatre producing works from the African diaspora. Non-Equity pay varies. Founded in 1999.*

Court Theatre

LORT D

5535 S. Ellis Ave.
Chicago, IL 60637
773/702-7005
773/753-4472 - Box Office
info@courttheatre.org
www.courttheatre.org
Artistic Director
Charles Newell
Executive Director
Dawn Helsing
Budget
$3 million
Nearest El
Garfield (Green Line) to 55th St. bus
Send Headshots to
Cree Rankin, Casting Director

> *Court Theatre discovers the power of classic theatre. Founded in 1954 as part of the University of Chicago.*

Drury Lane Oakbrook

FSy **⒭D** Special Agreement

100 Drury Lane
Oakbrook Terrace, IL 60181
630/570-7209
630/530-8300 - Box Office
bill.osetek@drurylaneoakbrook.com
www.drurylaneoakbrook.com
Artistic Director
William Osestek
Executive Director
Diane Van Lente
Nearest Public Transit
Elmhurst (Metra Union Pacific West)

> *Multiple Jeff-Award winner Drury Lane Oakbrook presents musical theatre to the Western suburbs. Founded in 1984.*

Theatres

Drury Lane Water Tower
CAT VI

> 175 E. Chestnut St.
> Chicago, IL 60611
> 312/642-2000 - Box Office
> *www.drurylanewatertower.com*
> *Executive Director*
> Jim Jensen
> *Nearest Public Transit*
> Chicago (Red Line)
>> *Drury Lane Water Tower started out in 2005 as a producing theatre, with season and artistic director. Six months later, they announced they would be a rental house.*

First Folio Shakespeare Festival
CAT III

> 146 Juliet Ct.
> Clarendon Hills, IL 60514
> 630/986-8067
> firstfolio@firstfolio.org
> *www.firstfolio.org*
> *Artistic Director*
> Alison Vesely
> *Managing Director*
> David Rice
> *Budget*
> $175,000
> *Send Headshots to*
> Alison Vesely
>> *Classics in the suburbs. Starting non-Equity pay is $75 a week. Founded in 1996.*

The Gift Theatre
E **ESc** **FD** CAT N

> 4802 N. Milwaukee Ave.
> Chicago, IL 60630
> 773/283-7071
> m.thornton@thegifttheatre.org
> *www.thegifttheatre.org*
> *Artistic Director*
> Michael Patrick Thornton
> *Managing Director*
> Rita Thornton
> *Executive Director*
> Daniel J. Ahlefeld
> *Nearest El*
> Jefferson Park (Blue Line)
> *Send Headshots to*
> Attn: Casting
>> *The Gift Theatre is dedicated to telling great stories on stage with honesty and simplicity. Since its 2002 debut, The Gift has consistently established itself as an actors' theatre, eschewing directorial cleverness for honest, powerful connections. Non-Equity pay is a $50 production stipend.*

Glitterati Productions
FSy CAT N

> 3635 W. Wrightwood Ave.
> Chicago, IL 60647
> 773/252-1895
> Glitteratiprods@aol.com
> *www.glitteratiproductions.com*
> *Artistic Director*
> John Nasca
> *Managing Director*
> Tiffany Nasca
> *Executive Director*
> Robert Hilliard
> *Send Headshots to*
> John Nasca
>> *The Glitterati producers are dedicated to the American art form of musical theatre and sophisticated comedies. Non-Equity pay varies. Founded in 2004.*

Goodman Theatre
ⒺSy **ⒼD** LORT B+ and LORT D

170 N. Dearborn St.
Chicago, IL 60601
312/443-3811
312/443-3800 - Box Office
www.goodmantheatre.org
Artistic Director
Robert Falls
Executive Director
Roche Schulfer
Budget
$16.3 million
Nearest Public Transit
State and Lake (Red, Orange,
Green, Blue, Pink, Purple Lines)
Send Headshots to
Adam Belcuore, Casting Director

Goodman Theatre is committed to producing classic and contemporary work,
giving full voice to a wide range of artists
and visions; central to that mission is the
Goodman Artistic Collective, including
Frank Galati, Mary Zimmerman, Chuck
Smith and Regina Taylor. Starting non-
Equity pay is $300 per week. Founded
in 1925 as part of the Art Institute;
1978 as a separate entity.

Illinois Theatre Center
ⒺSc CAT III

371 Artists Walk
Park Forest, IL 60466
708/481-3510
ilthctr@sbcglobal.net
www.ilthctr.org
Artistic Director
Etel Billig
Executive Director
Jonathan Billig
Budget
$510,000
Nearest Public Transit
Richton Park (Metra Electric)
Send Headshots to
Etel Billig

Illinois Theatre Center is the South
Suburbs' largest Equity theatre.
Starting non-Equity pay is $200 per
week. Founded in 1976.

Light Opera Works
Guest Artist

927 Noyes St., Suite 225
Evanston, IL 60201
847/869-7930
847/869-6300 - Box Office
info@light-opera-works.org
www.lightoperaworks.com
Artistic Director
Rudy Hogenmiller
Executive Director
Bridget McDonough
Budget
$1.3 million
Send Headshots to
Paige Keedy, Production Manager

Light Opera Works' mission is to produce
musical theatre from a variety of world traditions, to engage the community through
educational programs, and to train artists
in musical theatre. Starting non-Equity
pay is $300 per week. Founded in 1980.

Lookingglass Theatre Company
ⒾⒺ **ⒼD** CAT IV

821 N. Michigan Ave.
Chicago, IL 60611
773/477-9257
312/337-0665 - Box Office
info@lookingglasstheatre.org
www.lookingglasstheatre.org
Artistic Director
David Catlin
Managing Director
John Obligato
Executive Director
Rachel Kraft
Budget
$3.6 million
Nearest Public Transit
Chicago (Red Line)

Inventive, collaborative, and transfor-
mative, Lookingglass creates original,
story-centered theatre that seeks to
redefine the limits of theatrical experience. Starting non-Equity pay is $250
per week. Founded in 1988.

Theatres

Madison Repertory Theatre
SPT 10
> 1 S. Pinckney St., Suite 340
> Madison, WI 53703
> 608/256-0029
> *www.madisonrep.org*
> *Artistic Director*
> Richard Corley
> *Managing Director*
> Julie Jensen
> *Budget*
> $1.7 milliion
>> *Madison Rep is Madison, Wisconsin's regional anchor theatre. They hire lots of actors and designers from Chicago.*

Marriott Theatre
ESc RD Special Agreement
> 10 Marriott Dr.
> Lincolnshire, IL 60069
> 847/634-0204
> 847/634-0200 - Box Office
> *www.marriotttheatre.com*
> *Executive Director*
> Terry James
> *Nearest Public Transit*
> Buffalo Grove
> (Metra North Central Service)
> *Send Headshots to*
> Peter Sullivan, Artistic Administrator
>> *Run 52 weeks a year, theatre in the round, Marriott has 40,000 subscribers. Non-Equity pay is negotiated. Founded in 1976.*

Milwaukee Shakespeare Company
SPT 9
> 3073 S.Chase Ave., Building 28, Ste. 800
> Milwaukee, WI 53207
> 414/747-9662
> 414/747-9659 - Box Office
> *www.milwaukeeshakespeare.com*
> *Artistic Director*
> Paula Suozzi
> *Managing Director*
> Carrie Van Hallgren
>> *Milwaukee's Shakespeare theatre. They hire Chicago actors.*

Next Theatre Company
FSy CAT II
> 927 Noyes St.
> Evanston, IL 60201
> 847/475-1875
> info@nexttheatre.org
> *www.nexttheatre.org*
> *Artistic Director*
> Jason Loewith
> *Managing Director*
> John Collins
> *Budget*
> $550,000
> *Nearest Public Transit*
> Noyes (Purple Line)
> *Send Headshots to*
> Carmen Aiello, Casting Associate
>> *Next Theatre Company produces socially provocative, artistically adventurous work. Non-Equity pay is an honorarium. Founded in 1981.*

Noble Fool Theatricals
ꞡD CAT IV
> 4051 E. Main St.
> St. Charles, IL 60174
> 630/443-0438
> 630/585-6342 - Box Office
> info@noblefool.org
> *www.noblefool.org*
> *Artistic Director*
> John Gawlik
> *Managing Director*
> Colleen Tovar
>> *Noble Fool is the resident company of Pheasant Run resort in St. Charles. They previously had a space in the Loop, and before that were dedicated to sketch comedy based on improv.*

Northlight Theatre
Sy LORT D

9501 Skokie Blvd.
Skokie, IL 60077
847/679-9501
847/673-6300 - Box Office
info@northlight.org
www.northlight.org
Artistic Director
BJ Jones
Budget
$3.2 million
Nearest Public Transit
Skokie Stop (Yellow Line)
Send Headshots to
Lynn Baber, Artistic Administrator

> *Dedicated to enhancing the cultural life of the North Shore and Chicago, Northlight presents a diverse collection of new works and bold takes on classic texts which reflect and challenge the values and beliefs of the community it serves. Starting non-Equity pay is $300 per week. Founded in 1974.*

Oak Park Festival Theatre
CAT I

P.O. Box 4114
Oak Park, IL 60303
708/445-4440
festival@oakparkfestival.com
www.oakparkfestival.com
Artistic Director
Jack Hickey
Managing Director
Galen Gockel
Budget
$90,000
Nearest Public Transit
Harlem or Oak Park Ave. (Green Line)
Send Headshots to
Jack Hickey

> *Oak Park Festival is the Midwest's oldest professional theatre performing the classics outdoors and in. Non-Equity pay is $200 per production. Founded in 1975.*

Peninsula Players Theatre
⬛ E CORST Tier Z

4351 Peninsula Players Rd.
Fish Creek, WI 54212
920/868-3287
tickets@peninsulaplayers.com
www.peninsulaplayers.com
Artistic Director
Greg Vinkler
Executive Director
Todd Schmidt
Budget
$1.25 million
Send Headshots to
Greg Vinkler

> *America's oldest professional resident summer theatre. Non-Equity pay is $500 per week Founded in 1935.*

The Phoenix Theatre
Sy SPT II

749 N. Park Ave.
Indianapolis, IN 46202
317/635-2381
317/635-7529 - Box Office
tmcdonald@phoenixtheatre.org
www.phoenixtheatre.org
Producing Director
Bryan Fonseca
Managing Director
Sharon Gamble
Budget
$560,000
Send Headshots to
Bryan Fonseca

> *Phoenix is the only professional contemporary theatre in Indianapolis and does a number of Indiana, Midwest, and world premieres. Non-Equity pay is $150 per week. Founded in 1983.*

Piven Theatre Workshop
⬚Sc ⬚D CAT I

927 Noyes St.
Evanston, IL 60201
847/866-6597
847/866-8049 - Box Office
www.piventheatre.org
Artistic Director
Jennifer Green
Managing Director
Jennifer Sultz
Budget
$500,000
Nearest Public Transit
Noyes (Purple Line)
Send Headshots to
Andrew Bennett

> Piven does story theatre, melding various Methods with the work of Viola Spolin. They have trained John and Joan Cusack, Lili Taylor, Aiden Quinn and, of course, Jeremy Piven. Pay varies. Founded in 1971.

Porchlight Music Theatre Chicago
⬚Sy ⬚D CAT N

2814 N. Lincoln Ave.
Chicago, IL 60657
773/325-9884
773/327-5252 - Box Office
Porchlighttheatre@yahoo.com
www.porchlighttheatre.com
Artistic Director
L. Walter Stearns
Executive Director
Rhoda Reeling
Budget
$350,000
Send Headshots to
L. Walter Stearns

> Porchlight is Chicago's Music Theatre. By uniting the arts of music, drama, dance, and design they transform stories into thrilling, passionate and relevant events, which affect the lives of artists and audiences alike. Founded in 1994.

Provision Theater
⬚Sc CAT II

2211 N. Clybourn Ave., #2F
Chicago, IL 60614
773/506-4429
info@provisiontheater.org
www.provisiontheater.org
Artistic Director
Tim Gregory
Budget
$137,000
Send Headshots to
Tim Gregory

> Provision is devoted to producing works of hope, reconciliation and redemption; works that challenge us to explore a life of meaning and purpose. Non-Equity pay is a $250 stipend per production.

Remy Bumppo Theatre Company
⬚E ⬚Sy CAT II

3717 N. Ravenswood Ave., Suite 245
Chicago, IL 60613
773/244-8119
773/871-3000 - Box Office
info@remybumppo.org
www.remybumppo.org
Artistic Director
James Bohnen
Managing Director
Kristin Larsen
Budget
$700,000
Nearest Public Transit
Rehearsal space
Addison (Brown Line)
Send Headshots to
Linda Gillum, Casting Director

> Remy Bumppo's mission is to delight and engage audiences with the emotional and ethical complexities of society through the provocative power of great theatrical language. Non-Equity pay is a $100 per week. Founded in 1996.

Rivendell Theatre Ensemble
E **Sy** **D** CAT I

1711 W. Belle Plaine Ave. #3B
Chicago, IL 60613
773/472-1169
info@rivendelltheater.net
www.rivendelltheatre.net
Artistic Director
Tara Mallen
Executive Director
Chris Sanchez
Budget
$150,000
Send Headshots to
Tara Mallen

> RTE is committed to its mission of cultivating the talents of women theatre artists and to seeking out new plays that explore the unique female experience in an intimate, salon environment. Non-Equity pay is $500 per production. Founded in 1994.

Seanachai Theatre Company
E **ESc** **D** CAT I

2206 N. Tripp Ave.
Chicago, IL 60639
773/878-3727
info@seanachai.org
www.seanachai.org
Artistic Director
Jacquelyn Flaherty
Executive Director
Michael Grant
Budget
$40,000
Send Headshots to
Jacquelyn Flaherty, Artistic Director

> A Chicago theatre, steeped in the Irish storytelling tradition. Founded in 1995.

The Second City
E Special Agreement

1616 N. Wells St.
Chicago, IL 60614
312/664-4032
312/337-3992 - Box Office
sc1616@secondcity.com
www.secondcity.com
Managing Director
Jenna Altobelli
Executive Director
Andrew Alexander
Nearest Public Transit
Sedgwick (Brown Line)
Send Headshots to
Beth Kligerman, Director of Talent

> Since 1959, The Second City has established itself as a Chicago landmark and a national treasure, launching the careers of such comic greats as John Belushi, Mike Myers, Bill Murray, Gilda Radner, and more. Non-Equity pay varies from project to project. Founded Dec. 16, 1959.

The Shakespeare Project of Chicago
Sy **D** Stage D Reading

2529 W. Carmen Ave.
Chicago, IL 60625
773/334-8771
theshakespeareproject@att.net
www.shakespeareprojectchicago.org
Artistic Director
Jeff Christian
Executive Director
Mara Polster
Budget
$10,000
Send Headshots to
Jeff Christian

> Shakespeare Project is the only all-Equity company in the Midwest that is dedicated to performing text-based, actor-driven, free theatrical readings of Shakespeare and other great dramatists. No non-Equity pay. Founded in 1995.

Shattered Globe Theatre
E **ESc** **D** CAT I

2936 N. Southport Ave., Suite 210
Chicago, IL 60657
773/770-0333
773/871-3000 - Box Office
admin@shatteredglobe.org
www.shatteredglobe.org
Artistic Director
Brian Pudil
Managing Director
Elisa Spencer
Budget
$210,000
Nearest Public Transit
Fullerton (Brown/Red Line)
Send Headshots to
Brian Pudil, Artistic Director

Shattered Globe is an Jeff Award-winning theatre dedicated to great acting and ensemble work. Non-Equity pay is $50 per week. Founded in 1991.

ShawChicago Theater Company
Staged Reading

1016 N. Dearborn St.
Chicago, IL 60610
312/587-7390
312/409-5605 - Box Office
info@shawchicago.org
www.shawchicago.org
Artistic Director
Robert Scogin
Managing Director
Tony Courier
Budget
$230,000
Send Headshots to
Adrianne Cury, Artistic
Associate/Casting Director

ShawChicago presents concert readings of the plays of George Bernard Shaw and his contemporaries. Non-Equity pay depends on the show. Founded in 1994.

Steppenwolf Theatre Company
E **Sy** CAT various tiers

1650 N. Halsted St.
Chicago, IL 60614
312/335-1888
312/335-1650 - Box Office
www.steppenwolf.org
Artistic Director
Martha Lavey
Executive Director
David Hawkanson
Budget
Over $10 million
Nearest Public Transit
North/Clybourn (Red Line)
Send Headshots to
Erica Daniels, Casting Director

Committed to the principle of ensemble performance through the collaboration of a company of actors, directors and playwrights. Their three theatres are all on different Equity contracts. Non-Equity pay starts at $362.50 per week. Founded in 1976.

Teatro Vista...Theatre With A View
E CAT II

3712 N. Broadway, #275
Chicago, IL 60613
312/494-5767
diana@teatrovista.org
www.teatrovista.org
Artistic Director
Edward F. Torres
Managing Director
Diana Pando
Budget
$150,000 +
Send Headshots to
Charin Alvarez, Casting Director

Teatro Vista brings you some of the most provocative and edgy Latino writers in the U.S. and produces high quality productions, providing opportunities for directors, actors and designers. Non-Equity pay is $50 per production. Founded in 1989.

Theater Wit

ESc CAT II

1300 W Belmont Ave., #313
Chicago, IL 60657
312/375-1133
info@theaterwit.org
www.theaterwit.org
Artistic Director
Jeremy Wechsler
Managing Director
James Pelton
Budget
$90,000
Send Headshots to
Jeremy Wechsler

> Theater Wit is dedicated to producing
> new works of humor and intelligence
> to spark creative debate amongst its
> audience. Non-Equity pay is $100 per
> week. Founded in 2004.

Theatre at the Center

ESc CAT III

1040 Ridge Rd.
Munster, IN 46321
219/836-0422
219/836-3255 - Box Office
cgessert@comhs.org
www.theatreatthecenter.com
Artistic Director
William Pullinsi
Executive Direcctor
John Mybeck
Budget
$1.5 million
Send Headshots to
William Pullinsi

> The only professional, Equity theatre in
> Northwest Indiana. Founded in 1991.

TUTA Theatre Chicago

♪E CAT N

2032 W. Fulton St., Suite F-263-A
Chicago, IL 60612
773/680-0826
847/217-0691 - Box Office
info@tutato.com
www.tutato.com
Artistic Director
Zeljko Djukic
Managing Director
Natasha Djukic
Executive Director
Jacqueline Stone
Budget
$60,000
Send Headshots to
Zeljko Djukic

> TUTA's mission is to engage the
> American audience with relevant the-
> atre that is challenging in both form
> and content. Founded in 1996.

Victory Gardens Theater

ESc CAT IV

2257 N. Lincoln Ave.
Chicago, IL 60614
773/549-5788
773/871-3000 - Box Office
information@victorygardens.org
www.victorygardens.org
Artistic Director
Dennis Zacek
Managing Director
Marcelle McVay
Budget
$1.6 million
Nearest Public Transit
Fullerton (Brown, Red, Purple Lines)

> Dedicated to the playwright and the
> development of new work by diverse
> voices, Victory Gardens won the Regional
> Tony Award in 2001. Non-Equity pay
> starts at $257.50. Founded in 1974.

Theatres

Writers' Theatre

FSy CAT V

376 Park Ave.
Glencoe, IL 60222
847 / 242-6001
847 / 242-6000 - Box Office
info@writerstheatre.org
www.writerstheatre.org
Artistic Director
Michael Halberstam
Budget
$2.7 million

Nearest Public Transit
Glencoe (Metra Union Pacific North)
Send Headshots to
Jimmy McDermott, Artistic Assistant

> *Writers' Theatre is a professional company dedicated to a theatre of language and passion. The word and the artist are their primary focus. In their intimate environment, they offer productions that bring their audiences face-to-face with literature's greatest playwrights. Non-Equity pay starts at $250 per week. Founded in 1992.*

Theatres – Non-Equity

A Reasonable Facsimile Theatre Company

E ESc D

1225 W. Belmont Ave.
Chicago, IL 60657
773 / 282-9728
rengurl@yahoo.com
www.arftco.com
Artistic Director
Michael Buino
Managing Director
Jason Borkowski
Executive Director
Tina Haglund
Budget
$30,000
Send Headshots to
Tina Haglund, Executive Director,
4027 N. Laramie, Chicago, IL 60641

> *A Reasonable Facsimile focuses on New Works and Late Night theatre. No pay. Founded in 2000.*

The Actors Gymnasium

927 Noyes St.
Evanston, IL 60201
847/328-2795
admin@actorsgymnasium.com
www.actorsgymnasium.com
Artistic Director
Sylvia Hernandez-DiStasi
Executive Director
Larry DiStasi
Budget
$380,000
Nearest Public Transit
Noyes (Purple Line)

> *Actors Gym focuses on physical theatre and circus arts, and works closely with Lookingglass.*

Actors Workshop Theatre
⚑E **⬛Sy** **⬛D**

1044 W. Bryn Mawr St.
Chicago, IL 60660
773/728-7529 (PLAY)
colucci@actorsworkshop.org
www.actorsworkshop.org
Artistic Director
Michael Colucci
Managing Director
Jan Ellen Graves
Executive Director
Vaughn Fayle
Budget
$100,000
Nearest Public Transit
Bryn Mawr (Red Line)
Send Headshots to
Michael Colucci

> White hot drama in a tiny black box.
> No pay. Founded in 1994.

Aguijon Theater Company
⚑E **ESc** **⬛D**

2707 N. Laramie Ave.
Chicago, IL 60639
773/637-5899
info@aguijontheater.org
www.aguijontheater.org
Artistic Director
Rosario Vargas
Managing Director
Marcela Munoz
Budget
$75,000
Send Headshots to
Rosario Vargas

> Aguijon Theater Company of Chicago
> was founded in 1989 by Rosario Vargas
> and incorporated in 1990 as an inde-
> pendent, professional, non-profit the-
> atre company with the mission provid-
> ing quality Spanish language theatre
> to Latino and non-Latino audiences.
> Pay varies.

Albany Park Theater Project
⚑E

5100 N.Ridgeway Ave.
Chicago, IL 60625
773/866-0875
mail@aptpchicago.org
www.aptpchicago.org
Artistic Director
Laura Wiley
Executive Director
David Feiner
Budget
$500,000
Nearest Public Transit
Kimball (Brown Line)

> Albany Park Theater Project is is a
> multi-ethnic, ensemble-based theatre
> company of teens and young adults
> that creates original performance works
> based on the real-life stories of immi-
> grant and working-class Americans.
> Founded in 1996.

Albright Theatre Company
ESc

P.O. Box 61
Batavia, IL 60510
630/406-8838
info@albrighttheatre.com
www.albrighttheatre.com
Nearest Public Transit
Geneva (Metra Union Pacific West)
Send Headshots to
Casting Dept.

> A funky, edgy little suburban theatre
> that isn't afraid to take chances and
> has maintained the reputation for over
> 30 years of doing high quality produc-
> tions on a shoestring budget. Founded
> in 1973.

Theatres

Alchemy Theatre Company

350 S. Main St.
Lombard, IL 60148
630/766-2442
630/710-0915 - Box Office
alchemytheatre@yahoo.com
www.alchemytheatreco.com
Artistic Director
David Vogel
Managing Director
Kristin Collins
Budget
$28,000
Send Headshots to
David Vogel, Artistic Director

> *The mission of the Alchemy Theatre is to aspire for excellence in the creation of magical theatre while creating a trusting, safe, yet disciplined and professional environment. No pay. Founded in 2001.*

AlphaBet Soup Productions Childrens Theater

P.O. Box 85
Lombard, IL 60193
630/932-1555
info@absproductions.com
www.absproductions.com
Artistic Director
Susan Holm
Executive Director
Mark Pence
Send Headshots to
Casting

> *AlphaBet Soup Childrens Theater has spent 20 years building the theatre audience of the future while entertaining children between two and 102. Pay is $20 a performance. Founded in 1986.*

American Girl Place

111 E. Chicago Ave.
Chicago, IL 60611
312/787-3883
www.americangirl.com
Nearest Public Transit
Chicago (Red Line)
Send Headshots to
Casting

> *American Girls Theatre is part of the American Girl theme stores. They do two shows for girls-and their dolls. They regularly hire Chicago actors. Good pay.*

Appetite Theatre Company

900 W. Ainslie St., Unit H
Chicago, IL 60640
773/275-1931
info@appetitetheatre.com
www.appetitetheatre.com
Artistic Director
Michael Graham
Managing Director
Lauren Golanty
Executive Director
Liz Warton
Budget
$45,000
Send Headshots to
Michael Graham

> *Founded in 2004.*

Attic Playhouse

P.O. Box 10
Highland Park, IL 60040
847/433-2660
atticplay@aol.com
www.atticplayhouse.com
Artistic Director
Kimberly Loughlin
Send Headshots to
Kimberly Loughlin

> *Attic Playhouse, a professional, not-for-profit, 94-seat theatre is happy to be celebrating its ninth season. There is some pay.*

Babes With Blades
E **Sc** **D**

5920 N. Paulina St., #1W
Chicago, IL 60660
773/275-0440
business@babeswithblades.org
www.babeswithblades.org
Artistic Director
Dawn Alden
Managing Director
Amy Harmon
Budget
$45,000
Send Headshots to
Dawn Alden

> Babes With Blades expands opportunities for women by producing theatre that showcases their strength, vitality, and proficiency in the art of stage combat. Pay varies. Founded in 1997.

BackStage Theatre Company
E **Sc** **D**

P.O. Box 118142
Chicago, IL 60611
312/683-5347
info@backstagetheatrecompany.org
www.backstagetheatrecompany.org
Artistic Director
Brandon Bruce
Managing Director
Katherine Keberlein
Budget
$30,000
Send Headshots to
Brandon Bruce

> BackStage does big things in small spaces. No pay. Founded in 2000.

Bailiwick Repertory
Sc **D**

Bailiwick Arts Center
1229 W. Belmont Ave.
Chicago, IL 60657
773/883-1090
bailiwick@bailiwick.org
www.bailiwick.org
Artistic Director
David Zak
Managing Director
Lee Peters
Budget
$675,000
Nearest Public Transit
Belmont (Brown, Red, Purple Lines)
Send Headshots to
David Zak

> Bailiwick's programs reflect the diversity in which we live, with both classics and new works that are passionate, political, provocative. They do everything from gay theatre to theatre for the deaf to children's shows. They also rent space to all sorts ot theatre companies. They pay $20 per show. Founded in 1982.

Theatres

Barrel of Monkeys

⚼E

2936 N. Southport Ave.
Chicago, IL 60657
773/281-0638
312/409-1954 - Box Office
hthompson@barrelofmonkeys.org
www.barrelofmonkeys.org
Artistic Director
Halena Kays
Executive Director
Heidi Thompson
Budget
$276,000
Send Headshots to
Halena Kays

> Barrel of Monkeys (BOM) is an ensemble of actor/educators that creates an alternative learning environment in which children share their personal voices and celebrate the power of their imaginations through creative writing workshops and in-school and public performances. Pay is $80 per show. Founded in 1997.

Big Noise Theatre Company

515 E. Thacker St.
Des Plaines, IL 60016
847/604-0275
info@bignoisetheatre.org
www.bignoise.org
Artistic Director
Nancy Flaster

> Big Noise's mission is to produce high-quality shows that stretch the creative talents of actors and staff and surpass the expectations of audiences. Founded in 1972.

Blair Thomas & Company

3200 W. Carroll Ave.
Chicago, IL 60624
773/722-7248
blair@blairthomas.org
www.blairthomas.org
Artistic Director
Blair Thomas
Managing Director
Oriana Fowler
Budget
$175,000
Send Headshots to
Oriana Fowler

> Blair Thomas & Company creates puppet-based visual theatre. They frequently collaborate with other theatres, most recently Victory Gardens. Thomas is a founder of Redmoon Theatre. Founded in 2002.

Blue Heron Theatre

ESc RD

2010 Dewey Ave.
Evanston, IL 60201
847/392-0226
blueherontheatre@wowway.com
Artistic Director
Sheila Baker
Managing Director
Radica Radovic
Executive Director
Eileen Sutz
Budget
$20,000
Nearest Public Transit
Foster (Purple Line)
Send Headshots to
Sheila Baker

> Blue Heron's mission is to stage plays that explore multi-racial, multi-cultural issues in sensitive, thought-provoking ways and that celebrate life and the theatre. Pay varies. Founded in 2005.

Bohemian Theatre Ensemble
FSy **PD**

2437 W. Farragut Ave., #3B
Chicago, IL 60625
773/791-2393
info@bohotheatre.com
www.bohotheatre.com
Artistic Director
Stephen Genovese
Managing Director
Thomas Samorian
Send Headshots to
Stephen Genovese

> BoHo Theatre incoporates art as a
> whole; art for art's sake. Pay varies.
> Founded in 2003.

Caffeine Theatre
ESc

P.O. Box 1904
Chicago, IL 60690
773/561-7611
info@caffeinetheatre.com
www.caffeinetheatre.com
Artistic Director
Jennifer Shook
Send Headshots to
Jennifer Shook

> Caffeine mines the poetic tradition to
> explore social questions, celebrating
> poetry and examining poetry's relation-
> ship to society. Pay is $75 per produc-
> tion. Founded in 2003.

CenterLight Sign & Voice Theatre
ESc

614 Anthony Tr.
Northbrook, IL 60062
847/509-8260 ext.229
847/509-8260 ext.230 - Box Office
caschris@comcast.net
www.icodaarts.org
Executive Director
Christine Strejc
Budget
$350,000
Send Headshots to
Christine Strejc

> CenterLight Theatre uses deaf, and hard
> of hearing actors to perform all of
> our shows in American Sign Language
> and Spoken English. Alumni include
> Marlee Matlin.

C'est La Vie Drama

1140 N. LaSalle St., Suite 433
Chicago, IL 60610
888/539-4580
info@cestlaviedrama.org
www.cestlaviedrama.org
Artistic Director
Deborah Caruso

> C'est La Vie is what happens when
> MTV meets live theatre.

3 Theatres

Chase Park Theater

4701 N. Ashland Ave.
Chicago, IL 60640
773/750-7835
312/742-4701 - Box Office
karenfort@earthlink.net
www.chaseparktheater.org
Artistic Director
Karen Fort
Budget
$50,000
Nearest Public Transit
Lawrence (Red Line)
Damen (Brown Line)
Send Headshots to
Karen Fort

> *Classic theatre for a diverse community, Chase Park Theater works with many at-risk kids. No pay. Founded in 1960.*

Chemically Imbalanced Comedy
↕E

3406 N. Seminary Ave., #2
Chicago, IL 60657
773/865-7731
cicomedy@hotmail.com
www.cicomedy.com
Artistic Director
Farrell Walsh
Managing Director
Catherine Pappas
Executive Producer
Angela McMahon
Budget
$25,000
Send Headshots to
Angela McMahon

> *Chemically Imbalanced Comedy explores every aspect of Comedy through scripted and unscripted work, both original and previously produced. No pay. Founded in 2000.*

Chicago Kids Company– Theatre For Children

4104 N. Nashville Ave.
Chicago, IL 60634
773/205-9600
www.chicagokidscompany.com
Artistic Director
Jesus Perez
Executive Director
Paige Coffman
Budget
$500,000
Send Headshots to
Jesus Perez

> *Chicago Kids Company Theatre For Children produces modernized musical versions of classic fairy-tales, gearing shows for audiences ages 2 to 12. Pay is $30 per show. Founded in 1992.*

Chicago Opera Theater

70 E.Lake St., Suite 815
Chicago, IL 60601
312/704-8420
312/704-8414 - Box Office
info@chicagooperatheater.org
www.chicagooperatheater.org
General Director
Brian Dickie
Budget
$3 million
Nearest El
Randolph/Wabash (Brown Line)

Chicspeare Production Company
E

5751 N. Campbell Ave.
Chicago, IL 60659
773/699-2273
chicspeare@earthlink.net
www.chicspeare.org
Executive Director
Ann James
Budget
$30,000

> Chicspeare Production Company makes Shakespeare accessible to all Chicagoans through productions and educational programs. Their name reflects their commitment to both the city and Shakespeare's work. Pay is $60 a booking. Founded in 1996.

Chopin Theatre

1543 W. Division St.
Chicago, IL 60622
773/278-1500
www.chopintheatre.org
Nearest Public Transit
Ashland (Blue Line)
Executive Director
Zygmunt Dyrkacz

> Chopin produces theatre from Europe and rents space to Chicago companies.

Circle Theatre
Sc

7300 W. Madison St.
Forest Park, IL 60130
708/771-0700 ext. 1 - Box Office
info@circle-theatre.org
www.circle-theatre.org
Artistic Director
Kevin Bellie
Managing Director
Peter J. Storms
708/771-0700 ext. 3
Budget
$200,000
Nearest Public Transit
Harlem (Green Line)
Forest Park (Blue Line)
Send Headshots to
Kevin Bellie

> Circle Theatre is an artist-based company whose mission is to produce exciting and innovative theatre accessible to a widely diversified suburban and city audience. Pay is $200 a production. Founded in 1985.

Citadel Theatre
Sy D

P.O. Box 763
Lake Forest, IL 60045
847/735-8554
scottp@citadeltheatre.org
www.citadeltheatre.org
Artistic Director
Scott Phelps
Managing Director
Ann Bert
Budget
$50,000
Send Headshots to
Alexis Armstrong

> Located in Lake Forest on the North Shore, Citadel is a professional, not-for profit theatre dedicated to producing sophisticated, provocative work that will excite both the artist and the audience. Pay is $150 per production. Founded in 2002.

Theatres

City Lit Theater Co.

1020 W. Bryn Mawr Ave.
Chicago, IL 60660
773/293-3682
CityLitTheater@aol.com
www.citylit.org
Artistic Director
Terry McCabe
Managing Director
Brian Pastor
Budget
approx. $120,000
Nearest Public Transit
Bryn Mawr (Red Line)
Send Headshots to
Terry McCabe

> *City Lit does literate theatre, including adaptations of non-dramatic material such as novels, short stories, essays and poetry. The pay is $15 per performance. Founded in 1979.*

ComedySportz of Chicago

E

P.O. Box 25756
Chicago, IL 60625-0756
773/549-8080
boxoffice@comedysportzchicago.com
www.comedysportzchicago.com
Artistic Director
Dave Gaudet
Managing Director
Greg Werstler
Budget
$750,000 - $1 million
Send Headshots to
Dave Gaudet

> *ComedySportz of Chicago is an entertainment corporation that enriches lives and the creative imagination of the human spirit, by producing accessible, high-quality comedy. Founded in 1987.*

Corn Productions

E **ESc** **D**

4210 N. Lincoln Ave.
Chicago, IL 60618
773/868-0243
312/409-6435 - Box Office
Cornproductions@aol.com
www.cornservatory.org
Artistic Director
Robert Bouwman
Managing Director
Michelle Thompson-Hay
Budget
$65,000
Nearest Public Transit
Irving Park (Brown Line)
Send Headshots to
Jango Von Bebo, Casting Director

> *Corn does original mostly comedy works that tend toward the extreme. Brash, Bawdy, BYOB! No pay. Founded in 1992.*

DBA Studios

D

2540 N. Lincoln Ave.
Chicago, IL 60614
312/661-9100
info@dba-studios.com
www.dba-studios.com
Budget
$90,000
Send Headshots to
DBA Studios - Casting

> *DBA Studios creates new and provocative theatrical work, encouraging dialogue among races, cultures, and people. Pay is $15-$35 per show. Founded in 2003.*

DCA Theater (Department of Cultural Affairs)

78 E. Washington St.
Chicago, IL 60602
312/742-TIXS (8497) - Box Office
www.dcatheater.org
Artistic Director
Claire Sutton
Nearest Public Transit
Lake (Red Line)
Washington (Blue Line)
Randolph/Wabash (Brown Line)
Send Headshots to
DCA Theater does not accept headshots

> *The Chicago Department of Cultural Affairs Theatres (Storefront Theatre, Studio Theatre, Claudia Cassidy Theatre) offer downtown audiences the opportunity to experience Chicago's innovative off-Loop theatre companies, which are given residencies and other production opportunities.*

Democracy Burlesque
♟E **ᴱˢᶜ** **♟D**

5871 N. Glenwood Ave., #1
Chicago, IL 60660
773/275-4259
jafedorko@earthlink.net
www.democracyburlesque.com
Artistic Director
Joseph Fedorko
Send Headshots to
Joseph Fedorko

> *Democracy Burlesque is an interactive cabaret/revue/ happening/variety show for liberal and progressive artists, activists, and sympathizers. Any money made goes to political groups. Founded in 2006.*

Dog & Pony Theatre Company
♟E **ᶠˢʸ**

808 W Cuyler St., #2
Chicago, IL 60613
773/235-0492
dogandponytheatre@gmail.com
www.dogandponychicago.org
Artistic Director
Krissy Vanderwarker
Budget
$50,000
Send Headshots to
Krissy Vanderwarker

> *Dog & Pony produces new or lesser known work that is socially or politically relevant. Pay is $250 per production. Founded in 2002.*

Eclipse Theatre Company
♟E **♟D**

2000 W. Fulton St.
Chicago, IL 60612
312/409-1687
773/871-3000 - Box Office
info@eclipsetheatre.com
www.eclipsetheatre.com
Artistic Director
Anish Jethmalani
Managing Director
Thomas Jones
Budget
$85,000
Send Headshots to
Casting

> *Eclipse Theatre Company is the only Midwest theatre to feature the works of one playwright in one season. Founded in 1982.*

Emerald City Theatre

2936 N. Southport Ave.
Chicago, IL 60657
773 / 529-2690
773 / 935-6100 - Box Office
oz@emeraldcitytheatre.com
www.emeraldcitytheatre.com
Managing Director
Beth Klein
Executive Director
Karen Cardarelli
Budget
$100,000
Nearest El
Fullerton (Red/Brown Line)
Send Headshots to
Adam Fox, Associate Producer

> *Chicago's largest theatre specifically devoted to works for families and children. They produce shows at the Apollo Theatre on Lincoln, and work in schools. Pay varies per production. Founded in 1995.*

eta Creative Arts Foundation

7558 S. Chicago Ave.
Chicago, IL 60619
773 / 752-3955
email@etacreativearts.org
www.etacreativearts.org
Artistic Director
Runako Jahi
Executive Director
Abena Joan Brown
Budget
$1.1 million
Nearest Public Transit
79th (Red Line)
Send Headshots to
Runako Jahi

> *Eta tells African/African-American stories in the first voice. Pay is $30 per show. Founded in 1971.*

Factory Theater

3504 N. Elston Ave.
Chicago, IL 60618
312 / 409-3247
866 / 811-4111 - Box Office
chas@thefactorytheater.com
www.thefactorytheater.com
Artistic Director
Nick Digilio
Managing Director
Chas Vrba
Executive Director
Allison Cain
Nearest El
Addison (Blue Line)
Send Headshots to
Nick Digilio

> *Pay varies. Founded in 1994.*

Free Street

1419 W.Blackhawk Ave.
Chicago, IL 60622
773 / 772-7248
gogogo@freestreet.org
www.freestreet.org
Artistic Director
Ron Bieganski
Managing Director
Bryn Magnus
Budget
$250,000
Nearest Public Transit
Ashland (Blue Line)

> *Free Street Theater educates youth in its unique theatre process and creates original multi-media/non-autobiographical theatre pieces with youth. Pay is a stipend per production. Founded in 1969.*

Full Voice
[ESc]

P.O. Box 577948
Chicago, IL 60657
fullvoiceproductions@yahoo.com
www.fullvoice.org
Artistic Director
Cyra K. Polizzi
Managing Director
Richard Paro

> Full Voice projects question assumptions, often include multi-issue and gender/queer activism, and follow a vegan philosophy. Founded in 2002.

Galileo Players
[E]

1313 N. Ritchie Ct., Suite 903
Chicago, IL 60610
312/944-1986
info@galileoplayers.com
www.galileoplayers.com
Artistic Director
Tom Flanigan
Producer
Ronnie Feldman
Budget
$75,000
Send Headshots to
Ronnie Feldman

> The Galileo Players are a professional sketch comedy and improv troupe that focuses on scientific and philosophical themes. No pay. Founded in 2002.

Garrick Players Lake Forest College
[E] [ESc] [D]

555 Sheridan Rd.
Lake Forest, IL 60045
847/735-5141
847/735-5216 - Box Office
mae@lfc.edu
www.lakeforest.edu/academics/
programs/thtr/garrick
Artistic Director
Dennis Mae
Managing Director
Kate Witt
Executive Director
Heidi Anderson
Budget
$60,000
Nearest Public Transit
Lake Forest
(Metra Union Pacific North)

> Student-run college theatre.
> Do not send headshots.

GayCo Productions
[E]

5353 N. Magnolia Ave.
Chicago, IL 60640
773/989-5086
info@gayco.com
www.gayco.com
Budget
$35,000
Nearest Public Transit
Addison (Red Line)
Send Headshots to
Andrew Eninger, Talent Coordinator

> GayCo specializes in GLBT-themed sketch comedy where "gay" is the given, not the punchline. Pay is $25 per show. Founded in 1996.

Theatres

Gorilla Tango Theatre

1919 N. Milwaukee Ave.
Chicago, IL 60647
773/598-4549
info@gorillatango.com
www.gorillatango.com
Artistic Director
Daniel Abbate
Managing Director
Jeannie Petkewicz
Nearest Public Transit
Western (Blue Line)
Send Headshots to
Jeannie Petkewicz, General Manager
> GTT is a year-round for-profit theatre
> which features a variety of performers
> and performances on an ongoing basis.
> Founded in 2004.

Greasy Joan & Co.

2936 N. Southport Ave.
Chicago, IL 60657
312/458-0718
info@greasyjoan.org
www.greasyjoan.org
Artistic Director
Julieanne Ehre
Budget
approx. $50,000
Send Headshots to
Anna Weber, Associate Producer
> Greasy Joan & Co. re-imagines classic
> plays for the contemporary stage.
> Founded in 1995.

The GreyZelda Theatre Group

3729 N. Ravenswood Ave., Suite 138
Chicago, IL 60613
773/267-6293
greyzeldatheatre@yahoo.com
www.greyzelda.com or
www.myspace.com/greyzelda
Artistic Director
Rebecca Zellar
Managing Director
Derek Jarvis
Executive Director
Chris Riter
Budget
$15,000
Send Headshots to
Rebecca Zellar, co-artistic director
> Pay varies by show. Founded in 2004.

Griffin Theatre Company

3711 N.Ravenswood Ave.
Chicago, IL 60660
773/769-2228
773/327-5252 - Box Office
info@griffintheatre.com
www.griffintheatre.com
Co-Artistic Directors
Bill Massolia, Rick Barletta
Budget
$219,000
Send Headshots to
Rick Barletta
> The Griffin Theatre Company exists to
> create extraordinary and meaningful the-
> atrical experiences for both children and
> adults by building bridges of understand-
> ing between generations and instilling in
> its audience an appreciation of the per-
> forming arts. Pay varies per production.
> Founded in 1988.

The Grounded Theatre
ESc ⁛D

2618 Longview Dr.
Lisle, IL 60532
847/989-7927
630/739-3326 - Box Office
karen@groundedtheatre.org
www.groundedtheatre.org
Co-Artistic Director
David Lightner,
Co-Artistic Director
Karen Rosenberg,
Budget
varies
Send Headshots to
Karen Rosenberg

Professional, suburban not-for-profit theatre. Pay varies. Founded in 2000.

Grove Players

P.O. Box 92
Downers Grove, IL 60515
630/415-3682 - Box Office
www.groveplayers.org
Budget
$30-40,000
Nearest Public Transit
Downers Grove
(Metra Burlington Northern)

Grove Players takes pride in having truly open auditions, hiring new directors, and opening their doors to any volunteers who would like to be part of the team. Founded in 1936.

Halcyon Theatre
ESc ⁛D

1906 W. Winnemac Ave., #2
Chicago, IL 60640
312/458-9170
info@halcyontheatre.org
www.halcyontheatre.org
Artistic Director
Jennifer Adams
Executive Director
Tony Adams
Send Headshots to
Jennifer Adams

Founded in 2006.

HealthWorks Theatre
⁛Sy

2936 N. Southport Ave.
Chicago, IL 60657
773/929-4260
info@healthworkstheatre.org
www.healthworkstheatre.org
Artistic Director
Daren Leonard
Managing Director
Alex Miles Younger
Send Headshots to
Daren Leonard

Educational theatre for youth about health issues. Founded in 1988 to educate kids about AIDS.

Hell In A Handbag Productions
E **FSy** **RD**

1517 W. Rosemont Ave., #3E
Chicago, IL 60660-1322
312/409-4357
info@handbagproductions.org
www.handbagproductions.org
Artistic Director
David Cerda
Managing Director
Steve Hickson
Budget
approx. $50,000
Send Headshots to
Steve Hickson

> Hell in a Handbag Productions is dedi-
> cated to the preservation, exploration
> and celebration of works ingrained in the
> realm of popular culture via theatrical
> productions through parody, music and
> homage. Pay varies. Founded in 2002.

The House Theatre of Chicago
E **ESc**

4700 N. Ravenswood Ave., SW2
Chicago, IL 60640
773/769-3832
773/251-2195 - Box Office
info@thehousetheatre.com
www.thehousetheatre.com
Artistic Director
Nathan Allen
Executive Director
Phillip Klapperich
Budget
$300,000
Send Headshots to
Nathan Allen

> House is an ensemble of multi-talented
> artists who work together to create new
> works of popular theatre, which are
> very physical and presentational. Pay
> varies. Founded in 2001.

Hubris Productions
E **ESc** **FD**

724 W. Roscoe St., #3S
Chicago, IL 60657
773/398-3273
773/784-2772 - Box Office
pr@hubrisproductions.com
www.hubrisproductions.com
Artistic Director
Jacob Green
Executive Director
Anthony Guerrero
Send Headshots to
Jacob Green

> Hubris Productions embraces diversity
> and you never know what they are
> going to do next. Pay varies. Founded
> in 2005.

The Hypocrites
E

P.O. Box 578542
Chicago, IL 60657
312/409-5578
info@the-hypocrites.com
www.the-hypocrites.com
Artistic Director
Sean Graney
Managing Director
Mechelle Moe
Budget
$128,000
Send Headshots to
Geoff Button, Casting Director

> Striking a balance between unyielding
> emotional honesty and high theatrical-
> ity. Stipend available. Founded in 1997.

Imagination Theater

4802 N. Broadway, #201-B
Chicago, IL 60640
773/303-0070
info@imaginationtheater.org
www.imaginationtheater.org
Artistic Director
Steve Leaver
Budget
$278,000
Nearest Public Transit
Lawrence (Red Line)
Send Headshots to
Steve Leaver

> *Imagination Theater is a touring company using interactive theatre techniques to address various social issues for audiences of all ages. Pay is $11 per hour. Founded in 1966.*

Infamous Commonwealth Theatre
ESc **D**

4845 N. Harding Ave., Unit 1
Chicago, IL 60625
312/458-9780
info@infamouscommonwealth.org
www.infamouscommonwealth.org
Artistic Director
Genevieve Thompson
Managing Director
Diane Fairchild
Budget
$43,000
Send Headshots to
Genevieve Thompson

> *Infamous Commonwealth Theatre's unique mission is to illuminate diverse perspectives around one centralized topic per season using contrasting theatrical styles. Pay is $40 per production. Founded in 2001.*

iO (Formerly Improv Olympic)

3541 N. Clark St.
Chicago, IL 60657
773/880-0199
info@iochicago.net
www.iochicago.net
Artistic Director
Charna Halpern
Managing Director
Michael Click
Nearest Public Transit
Addison (Red Line)
Send Headshots to
Charna Halpern

> *iO is the theatre that's famous for creating long form improvisation and the school that has nurutured some of the world's greatest comedic talents in Hollywood. No pay. Founded in 1981.*

Janus Theatre Company
Sy **D**

919 Prospect Blvd.
Elgin, IL 60120
847/841-1713
info@janustheatre.org
www.janustheatre.org
Artistic Director
Terry Domschke
Managing Director
Sean Hargadon
Budget
$50,000
Send Headshots to
Sean Hargadon

> *Janus Theatre Company produces work that is stripped of any frills, leaving just the actor, the audience, and the play to connect collectively in the empty space. Pay is $100 per production. Founded in 1998.*

Theatres

Jedlicka Performing Arts Center
[=Sy]

3801 S.Central Ave.
Cicero, IL 60804
708/656-3948 - Box Office
www.jpactheatre.com
Producer
Joseph Messina
Executive Director
Dante Orfei
708/656-8000 ext.273
Nearest Public Transit
54th (Blue Line)
Send Headshots to
Joseph Messina

> The Jedlicka Performing Arts Center is
> known for its large-scale productions
> and highly affordable tickets, which
> make vibrant theatre accessible to all.

The Journeymen
[=Sy] [=D]

3915 N. Janssen Ave.
Chicago, IL 60613
773/857-5395
773/857-5395 - Box Office
thejourneymen@aol.com
www.thejourneymen.com
Artistic Director
Frank Pullen
Budget
$150,000
Send Headshots to
Frank Pullen

> The Journeymen are dedicated to multi-
> cultural education through artistic
> exchange. Pay varies. Founded in 1994.

Keyhole Theatre
[E] [=Sy]

1500 N. Bell Ave.
Chicago, IL 60622
773/805-5055
keyholetheatre@comcast.net
www.keyholetheatre.com
Artistic Director
Frank Merle
Managing Director
Erin Killean
Budget
$15,000
Nearest Public Transit
Damen (Blue Line)
Send Headshots to
Frank Merle

> Keyhole is dedicated to producing high
> quality, affordable theatre that provides
> an intimate look at the human experi-
> ence, as if secretly looking "through a
> keyhole" at scenes and characters that
> capture the essence of the human heart
> and soul. Small stipend available.
> Founded in 1999.

Kidworks Touring Theatre Co.
[E] [=Sy] [=D]

5215 N. Ravenswood Ave., #307
Chicago, IL 60640
773/907-9932
Kidworkstheatre@aol.com
www.kidworkstheatre.org
Artistic Director
Andrea Salloum
Budget
$95,000
Send Headshots to
Andrea Salloum

> Kidworks celebrates its 20th season
> opening the doors between education
> and imagination and bringing litera-
> ture, geography and history to life. Most
> of their work is in schools. Pay is $50
> per show. Founded in 1987.

Lifeline Theatre
⏺E

6912 N. Glenwood Ave.
Chicago, IL 60626
773/761-0667
casting@lifelinetheatre.com
www.lifelinetheatre.com
Artistic Director
Dorothy Milne
Managing Director
Vivienne Dipeolu
Budget
$500,000
Nearest Public Transit
Morse (Red Line)
Send Headshots to
Robert Kauzlaric, Casting Director

> *Lifeline does literary adaptations for children and adults. They also do off-school workshops for 2nd-6th graders (Columbus Day, Presidents Day, Martin Luther King Day, etc.)*

Live Bait Theater
⏺Sc ⏺D

3914 N. Clark St.
Chicago, IL 60613
773/871-1212
aaron@livebaittheater.org
www.livebaittheater.org
Artistic Director
Sharon Evans
Managing Director
Aaron Johnson
Executive Director
John Ragir
Budget
$250,000
Nearest Public Transit
Addison (Red Line)
Send Headshots to
Sharon Evans

> *Live Bait Theater produces several original works annually as well as providing two rental spaces to the greater theatre community. Founded in 1987.*

LiveWire Chicago Theatre
⏺Sc ⏺D

1100 N. Dearborn Ave., #1509
Chicago, IL 60611
773/412-8089
www.livewirechicago.com
Artistic Director
Glenn Proud
Managing Director
Chris Dennis
Send Headshots to
Glenn Proud

> *Pay is a stipend. Founded in 2003.*

Mary Arrchie Theatre
⏺E

731 W. Sheridan Rd.
Chicago, IL 60613
773/871-0442
coyotesky2000@sbcglobal.net
www.maryarrchie.com
Artistic Director
Richard Cotovsky
Producing Director
Hans Fleischmann
Nearest Public Transit
Sheridan (Red Line)

> *In addition to its regular shows, Mary Arrchie produces the Abbie Hoffman Died For Our Sins festival in their tiny space. Founded in 1986.*

Theatres

Metropolis Performing Arts Centre

111 W.Campbell St.
Arlington Heights, IL 60005
847/577-5982
847/577-2121 - Box Office
info@metropolisarts.com
www.metropolisarts.com
Executive Director
Tim Rater
Budget
$2.5 million
Nearest Public Transit
Arlington Heights
(Metra Union Pacific North)
Send Headshots to
Dan Gildersleeve, Production Manager

Metropolis is truly a Performing Arts Centre offering over 50 different shows/ artists in over 400 performances in 365 days. They both present other theatre companies and produce. Pay is $150 per week. Founded in 2000.

The Mill (aka Experimental Theatre Chicago)

1738 W. Gregory St.
Chicago, IL 60640
312/388-7660
info@themilltheatre.org
www.themilltheatre.org
Artistic Director
Jaclyn Biskup
Budget
$10,000-$18,000
Send Headshots to
Jaclyn Biskup

The Mill makes work that is progressive in form and content. No pay. Founded in 2002.

MOB Productions

4741 N. Artesian Ave. #3
Chicago, IL 60625
MOBProductions@gmail.com
www.mobproductions.org
Artistic Director
Alex Goodman
Managing Director
Elliot Hirsen
Budget
$30,000
Send Headshots to
MOBProductions@gmail.com

MOB Productions locally reimagines popular culture. Founded in 2005.

The Moving Dock Theatre Company

410 S. Michigan Ave., Suite #720
Chicago, IL 60605
312/427-5490
contact@movingdock.org
www.movingdock.org
Artistic Director
Dawn Arnold
Send Headshots to
Dawn Arnold

The Moving Dock Theatre Company creates new work and reinterprets established scripts through its focus on the actor's creative process. Founded in 1997.

MPAACT

P.O. Box 10039
Chicago, IL 60610
312/409-6724
773/871-3000 - Box Office
info@mpaact.org
www.mpaact.org
Executive Director
Reginald Lawrence
Send Headshots to
LaNisa Frederick

MPAACT produces Afrikan Centered Theatre: original and innovative works by writers from the African diaspora that explore our experiences in all its complexity often with the use of live music and/or movement. Founded in 1992.

Mystery Shop
♟E **ESc**

551 Sundance Ct.
Carol Stream, IL 60188
630/690-1105
tms@themysteryshop.com
www.themysteryshop.com
Artistic Director
Mary Heitert
Send Headshots to
Mary Heitert

> *Traveling theatre specializes in adult and
> children's interactive mysteries and programs.
> Pay is $40 per show. Founded in 1988.*

n.u.f.a.n. ensemble
♟E **ESc** **D**

4261 W. Addison St.
Chicago, IL 60641
773/282-0344
nufanensemble@sbcglobal.net
www.nufanensemble.com
Artistic Director
Paul Barile
Managing Director
John Champion
Budget
varies
Send Headshots to
Paul Barile

> *Chicago world premieres by Chicago play-
> wrights. Pay varies. Founded in 2004.*

The Neo-Futurists
♟E

5153 N. Ashland Ave.
Chicago, IL 60640
773/878-4557
773/275-5255 - Box Office
info@neofuturists.org
www.neofuturists.org
Artistic Director
Sharon Greene
Budget
$450,000
Nearest Public Transit
Berwyn (Red Line)

> *The Neo-Futurists perform with their
> own unique aesthetic (Neo-Futurism) in
> which they neither play characters nor
> aim to suspend the audience's disbelief.
> Pay for ensemble members is $100 per
> week. Founded in 1988.*

New Branch Theatre Company
ESc **D**

P.O. Box 87177
Chicago, IL 60680
312/458-0702
newbranchtheatre@mail.com
www.newbranchtheatre.com
Artistic Director
Patricia Sykes
Managing Director
Ansonia Gibbs
President
Calvin Gibbs
Budget
$500,000
Send Headshots to
Calvin Gibbs

> *New Branch produces all genres of the-
> atre, have a repetoire of shows suitable
> for dinner theatre and do an annual
> Christian show. Pay is $50 per show.
> Founded in 2003.*

Theatres

New Leaf Theatre
ESc D

1225 W. Chase Ave., #F2
Chicago, IL 60626
773/274-9026
newleaf@newleaftheatre.org
www.newleaftheatre.org
Artistic Director
Brandon Ray
Managing Director
Tanya Ray
Budget
$23,000
Nearest Public Transit
Armitage (Brown Line)
Fullerton (Red Line)
Send Headshots to
Brandon Ray

> *New Leaf Theatre creates intimate, animate theatrical experiences which renew both artist and audience. No pay. Founded in 2001.*

New Millennium Theatre Company
Sy

5043 W. Deming Pl.
Chicago, IL 60639
773/989-4515
info@nmtchicago.org
www.nmtchicago.org
Artistic Director
Chad Wise
Managing Director
Zenna Wise
Executive Director
Pete Guither
Budget
$30,000
Send Headshots to
Chad Wise

> *New Millennium does shows that they, as 20- and 30-somethings, would want to see: pop-culture based entertainment that appeals to regular theatre-goers and Average Joe Stock Trader and his girlfriend. Pay varies. Founded in 1998.*

New World Repertory Theater
E Sy

923 Curtiss St.
Downers Grove, IL 60515
630/663-1489
info@newworldrep.org
www.newworldrep.org
Artistic Director
Jean Gottlieb
Managing Director
Alison Henderson
Budget
$50,000
Nearest Public Transit
Main Street-Downers Grove
(Metra BNSF)
Send Headshots to
Jean Gottlieb

Open Eye Productions
E Sy D

1800 W. Cornelia Ave., Suite 111
Chicago, IL 60657
773/510-7748
oep_rentals@yahoo.com
www.openeyeproductions.org
Artistic Director
Chris Maher
Executive Director
Jon Sevigny
Send Headshots to
Chris Maher

> *Open Eye Productions is an ensemble-based theatre company dedicated to the exploration of human eccentricities, pursuing humor and honesty above all else. No pay. Founded in 1996.*

Ouroboros Theatre Company
⬤E **ESc** **PD**

1537 Grove Ave.
Berwyn, IL 60402
708/254-0928
lara@ouroborostheatre.com
www.ouroborostheatre.com
Artistic Director
Lara Filip-Tibble
Managing Director
Jenni Sumerak
Send Headshots to
Lara Filip-Tibble

> The Mission of Ouroboros is to perpetu-
> ate the art of story telling through live
> theatre. Pay varies. Founded in 2004.

Pegasus Players

1145 W. Wilson Ave.
Chicago, IL 60640
773/878-9761
alex@pegasusplayers.org
www.pegasusplayers.org
Artistic Director
Alex Levy
Managing Director
Katie Klemme
Executive Director
Arlene Crewdson
Budget
$650,000
Nearest Public Transit
Wilson (Red Line)
Send Headshots to
Alex Levy

> Pegasus Players builds community in
> Uptown's diverse neighborhood with
> four mainstage productions and exten-
> sive outreach programming, including
> their annual Young Playwrights Festival.
> Pay is $120 a week. Founded in 1978.

Piccolo Theatre
⬤E **FSy**

600 Main St.
Evanston, IL 60202
847/424-0089
info@piccolotheatre.com
www.piccolotheatre.com
Artistic Director
John Szostek
Budget
$50,000
Nearest Public Transit
Main (Purple Line)
Main (Metra Union Pacific North)
Send Headshots to
David Kelch, Casting Director

> The Piccolo Theatre Ensemble embodies
> and realizes the human comedy
> through physical theatre, eloquence
> and humor in order to move, delight
> and transform audiences. Pay is an
> honorarium. Founded in 2000.

Pine Box Theatre
⬤E **FSy** **PD**

P.O. Box 180054
Chicago, IL 60618
info@pineboxtheatre.org
www.pineboxtheatre.org
Co-Artistic Directors
Anne Adams, Audrey Francis
Managing Director
Laura Hooper
Budget
$40,000
Send Headshots to
Audrey Francis

> Pine Box Theatre is an ensemble of
> friends who graduated from the School
> at Steppenwolf. They strive to tell sto-
> ries not from one perspective, but from
> all perspectives. Founded in 2004.

Theatres

Plasticene

2122 N. Winchester Ave.
Chicago, IL 60614
312/409-0400
dexter@plasticene.com
www.plasticene.com
Artistic Director
Dexter Bullard
Budget
$60,000
Send Headshots to
Dexter Bullard

> Plasticene is an ensemble dedicated to
> creating original high impact collabora-
> tive physical theatre constructed from
> the resources of research, objects,
> bodies, light, sound, and projections.
> Pay is $400 per show. Founded in 1995.

Players Ring Theatre

3501 N. Southport Ave., #328
Chicago, IL 60657
773/857-0561
playersring@playersringwest.org
www.playersringwest.org
Artistic Director
Michael Gillett
Managing Director
Katherine Wray
Executive Director
Barbara Newton
Budget
$25,000
Send Headshots to
Michael Gillett

> Payers Ring Theatre seeks to present
> rarely produced scripts, published or
> original, with special emphasis on
> scripts first workshopped and produced
> at The Players' Ring of Portsmouth, NH.
> No pay. Founded in 2005.

The Playground Theater

3209 N. Halsted St.
Chicago, IL 60657
312/961-9477
773/871-3793 - Box Office
matt@the-playground.com
www.the-playground.com
Executive Director
Matt Barbera
Nearest Public Transit
Belmont (Brown and Red Lines)

> The Playground Theater is an impro-
> viser/actor run cooperative theatre
> whose main focus is the perfomance
> of improvisational comedy. Founded
> in 1997.

Point of Contention Theatre Company [POC]

655 W. Irving Park Rd., #509
Chicago, IL 60613
630/220-0730
pointofcontention@hotmail.com
Artistic Director
Jamie DesRocher
Managing Director
Robert Bullen
Executive Director
Lindsey MacAllister
Send Headshots to
Lindsey MacAllister

> Through a wide range of repertoire,
> POC provides a forum from which the
> community at large can interpret, dis-
> cuss, and better understand their lives
> and the world in which they live. No
> pay. Founded in 2006.

Polarity Ensemble Theatre
♠ E FSy ℘D

135 Asbury Ave.
Evanston, IL 60202
847/475-1139
847/293-7705 - Box Office
richard@richardengling.com
www.petheatre.com
Artistic Director
Richard Engling
Managing Director
Ann Keen
Executive Director
Richard Engling
Budget
under $15,000
Send Headshots to
Richard Engling

> Polarity Ensemble Theatre focuses on creating innovative productions of classical work and definitive productions of original work by local playwrights. They publish some of the work they produce. Pay varies. Founded in 2004.

Premiere Theatre & Performance
FSy ℘D

2936 N. Southport Ave.
Chicago, IL 60647
773/250-7055
patrizia@ptapchicago.org
www.ptapchicago.org
Artistic Director
Patrizia Acerra

> Premiere Theatre and Performance (formerly the International Theatre of Chicago) creates and produces director-driven original works, translations and adaptations. No pay. Founded in 2003.

pretty blue sky
ESc ℘D

6030 N. Sheridan Rd., #812
Chicago, IL 60660
773/334-0739
catherine@prettybluesky.com
www.prettybluesky.com/skytheater.html
Artistic Director
Bridget Kies
Director Of Theatre
Catherine Hermes
Send Headshots to
Catherine Hermes

> Whether contemporary or classic, intimate or spectacle, their goal is to produce aesthetically beautiful work with form of equal importance to its content. Pay varies. Founded in 2006.

Profiles Theatre
♠ E FSy ℘D

4147 N. Broadway
Chicago, IL 60613
773/549-1815
profilesco@aol.com
www.profilestheatre.org
Artistic Director
Joe Jahraus
Managing Director
Darrell W. Cox
Budget
$60,000
Nearest Public Transit
Wilson or Sheridan (Red Line)
Send Headshots to
Darrell W. Cox

> Profiles Theatre's primary goal is to bring new works to Chicago that illuminate the determination and resiliency of the human spirit. Pay varies. Founded in 1988.

Theatres

Promethean Theatre Ensemble

⬤E **⬤D**

808 Junior Ter., #506
Chicago, IL 60613
847/452-3352
www.prometheantheatre.org
Artistic Director
Stephen F. Murray
Executive Director
Brian Pastor
Send Headshots to
Tom Weber

> Promethean Theatre Ensemble empha-
> sizes strong, courageous storytelling,
> accessible ticket prices, and proposes in
> its mission to "present gifts of language
> and imagery bound together into living,
> breathing performances."

Prop Thtr

⬤Sc **⬤D**

3502-04 N. Elston Ave.
Chicago, IL 60618
773/539-7804
773/539-7838 - Box Office
info@propthtr.org
www.propthtr.org
Co-Artistic Directors
Scott Vehill, Stefan Brun
Managing Director
Don Schroeder
Executive Director
Diane Honeyman-Bloede
Budget
$150,000
Nearest Public Transit
Belmont (Blue Line)
Send Headshots to
Diane Honeyman-Bloede

> Chicago's founding member of the
> National New Play Network, Prop Thtr
> promotes new work and young theater
> professionals. Pay is $15 - $25 per
> show. Founded in 1981.

Quest Theatre Ensemble

⬤E **⬤Sc** **⬤D**

1609 W. Gregory St.
Chicago, IL 60640
312/458-0895
info@questensemble.org
www.questensemble.org
Artistic Director
Andrew Park
Managing Director
Jason Bowen
Executive Director
Amanda Church
Nearest Public Transit
Bryn Mawr (Red Line)
Send Headshots to
Jason Bowen, Managing Director

> Quest Theatre Ensemble tells familiar
> stories in a new way using spectacle,
> large scale puppetry and music. Quest
> Theatre offers all productons free of
> charge so that no one is excluded. Pay is
> $100 per production. Founded in 2002.

Rasaka Theatre Company

⬤E **⬤Sc** **⬤D**

2936 N. Southport Ave.
Chicago, IL 60657
312/777-1070
info@rasakatheatre.org
www.rasakatheatre.org
Artistic Director
Anish Jethmalani
Managing Director
Mary Anne Mohanraj
Budget
$50,000
Send Headshots to
Anish Jethmalani

> Rasaka provides a platform for South
> Asian artists to perform, be challenged
> and to develop as artists. They also
> serve the theatre-going community as
> a vehicle for education on South Asian
> and diaspora culture. Pay is $100
> a production. Founded in 2004.

Rascal Children's Theater
⌗E ⌗Sc ⌗D

5123 N. Clark St.
Chicago, IL 60640
773/561-5893
dan@comcast.net
www.roguetheater.com
Artistic Director
Dan Foss
Nearest Public Transit
Argyle (Red Line) or #22 Clark bus
Send Headshots to
Dan Foss

> Rascal is the children's theatre of Rogue Theatre. No pay. Founded in 2006.

Raven Theatre
⌗E ⌗Sc

6157 N. Clark St.
Chicago, IL 60660
773/338-2177
raventheatre@aol.com
www.raventheatre.com
Artistic Director
Michael Menendian
Managing Director
JoAnn Montemurro
Budget
$350,000
Nearest Public Transit
Granville (Red Line)
Send Headshots to
Frank Merle, Administrative Manager

> Raven focuses on projects that illuminate the American experience through classics and lesser known works of the American stage. Pay is a stipend that varies. Founded in 1983.

Red Jacket Theatre Company
⌗E ⌗Sy ⌗D

2318 N. Southport Ave., #1R
Chicago, IL 60614
312/493-9561
www.redjackettheatre.com
Artistic Director
Andrew Perez
Managing Director
Blake Merriman
Executive Director
Sarra Kaufman
Budget
$10,000
Send Headshots to
Jonny Sanders, Ensemble Member

> Red Jacket is an ensemble-driven theatre company striving to revivify American theatre for a new generation through world premieres and charged productions of classics. No pay. Founded in 2004.

Redmoon Theater

1438 W. Kinzie St.
Chicago, IL 60622
312/850-8440
312/850-8440 ext.111 - Box Office
information@redmoon.org
www.redmoon.org
Artistic Director
Jim Lasko
Managing Director
Christy Uchida
Budget
$2 million
Nearest Public Transit
Ashland (Green Line)

> Redmoon transforms public spaces into places of celebration through the creation of spectacle theatre, a highly visual and inventive theatre style that embraces the act of transformation through pageantry, puppetry and contraption-type mechanical objects. Pay is a stipend. Founded in 1989.

Theatres

The Rescuers

2214 N. Leavitt St., #2F
Chicago, IL 60647
312/972-0045
RescuersTheater@gmail.com
Artistic Director
Sharon Lanza
Managing Director
Andrea Mustain
Send Headshots to
Sharon Lanza
>Founded in 2005.

REVOLUTION Theatre Company

28 E. Jackson Blvd., Ste.10-R565
Chicago, IL 60604
312/494-2675
revolutiontheatrechicago@yahoo.com
www.revolutiontheatre.org
Artistic Director
John Thurner
Managing Director
Michelle Jones
Send Headshots to
Casting
>*Revolution produces work by up-and-coming playwrights on the cutting edge. No pay. Founded in 2002.*

The Right Brain Project

4331 N. Ashland Ave., Apt. 3
Chicago, IL 60613
773/474-2599
therbp@gmail.com
Artistic Director
Nathan Robbel
Managing Director
Colby Sellers
Executive Director
Anthony Ingram
Budget
Approx. $15,000+
Send Headshots to
Anthony Ingram
>*The RBP focuses on the collaborative nature of theatre, while delivering rarely seen and unique works that are important and pertinent to our times. No pay. Founded in 2005.*

Rogue Theater

5123 N. Clark St.
Chicago, IL 60640
773/561-5893
rogue@roguetheater.com
www.roguetheater.com
Artistic Director
Nate White
Nearest Public Transit
Argyle (Red Line) or #22 Clark Bus
Send Headshots to
Dan Foss
>*Rogue produces affordable, gender-balanced theatre about rogues, rebels, misfits and outcasts. No pay. Founded in 2002.*

Rubicon Theatre Project

1610 W. Sunnyside Ave., Unit 1W
Chicago, IL 60640
773/275-2065
rubicontheatreproject@yahoo.com
www.rubicontheatreproject.org
Budget
$10,000
Send Headshots to
Kassi Dallmann, Secretary

> *While remaining flexible with their repertory, staging, and design, Rubicon presents theatre that reflects and responds to our ever-changing culture and examines the complexities of the human condition. No pay. Founded in 2005.*

Saint Sebastian Players
Sc

c/o St. Bonaventure
1625-1641 W. Diversey Pkwy.
Chicago, IL 60613
773/404-7922
stsebplyrs@aol.com
President
Jonathan Hagloch
Treasurer
Jim Masini
Budget
$15,000
Nearest Public Transit
Diversey (Brown Line)

> *Saint Sebastian Players produces plays and musicals, original audience-participation murder mysteries and the annual Monologue Matchup Competition. No pay. Founded in 1982.*

Sansculottes Theater Company

P.O. Box 256570
Chicago, IL 60625-6570
info@sansculottes.org
www.sansculottes.org
Artistic Director
Tom Horan
Budget
$10,000
Send Headshots to
Elizabeth Bagby

> *Sansculottes Theater Company produces original work that challanges the status quo. No pay. Founded in 2003.*

Schadenfreude
E

4636 N. Ravenswood Ave.
Chicago, IL 60640
773/576-6070
info@schadenfreude.net
www.schadenfreude.net
Artistic Director
Sandy Marshall
Managing Director
Stephen Schmidt
Executive Director
Kate James
Budget
approx. $20,000

> *Schadenfreude is Chicago's independent sketch comedy ensemble. Founded in 1997.*

Theatres

Sense of Urgency Productions

905 S. Grove Ave., 1st Floor
Oak Park, IL 60304
708/267-9845
keitel@elmhurst.edu
www.senseofurgency.org
Artistic Director
Edwin Wilson
Budget
$19,500
Send Headshots to
Edwin Wilson

> As Sense of Urgency continues to evolve,
> they look to explore other mediums like
> film prodction, education and community
> outreach. Pay varies. Founded in 1995.

Serendipity Theatre Collective

2936 N. Southport Ave.
Chicago, IL 60647
773/296-0163
lauren@serendipitytheatre.org
www.serendipitytheatre.org
Artistic Director
Lauren Pesca
Managing Director
Amy Brown
Budget
$60,000
Send Headshots to
Matt Miller, Casting Director

> Serendipity Theatre Company seeks to
> intiate and provide a forum for social
> dialogue through the creation of theatri-
> cal productions. Pay is negotiable.
> Founded in 1999.

Shantz Theatre

4235 N. Bell Ave.
Chicago, IL 60618
773/369-8566
matt@shantztheatre.com
www.shantztheatre.com
Artistic Director
Matt Fotis
Managing Director
Jeanette Nielsen
Executive Director
Bill Wanderer
Budget
Less than $50,000
Send Headshots to
Matt Fotis

> Shantz Theatre is dedicated to produc-
> ing original works that explore the
> human condition through humor and
> that stretch traditional notions of narra-
> tive storytelling. Pay is a $150 stipend
> per production. Founded in 2002.

the side project

1439 W. Jarvis Ave.
Chicago, IL 60626
773/973-2150
adam@thesideproject.net
www.thesideproject.net
Artistic Director
Adam Webster
Budget
$35,000
Nearest Public Transit
Jarvis (Red Line)
Send Headshots to
Adam Webster

> The side project strives to apply its
> hyper-intimate use of space to redefine
> immediacy in the theatre in order to
> expose in sharp detail the delicate inter-
> workings of humanity's vulnerability and
> resiliency. Pay varies. Founded in 2000.

Signal Ensemble Theatre
⚫E **⟱Sy**

P.O. Box 199, 3023 N. Clark St.
Chicago, IL 60657
773/347-1350
info@signalensemble.com
www.signalensemble.com
General Artistic Director
Ronan Marra
Managing Director
Joseph Stearns
Executive Director
Christopher Prentice
Budget
$60,000
Send Headshots to
Ronan Marra

> Signal Ensemble Theatre is known for
> its ensemble acting and producing a
> diverse slate of plays that range from
> classics to new works, Signal is an
> actor's theatre. Pay is $10 per show.
> Founded in 2002.

Silk Road Theatre Project
≣Sc **⟱D**

77 W. Washington St., Pierce Hall
Chicago, IL 60602
312/857-1234 ext. 204
312/857-1234 ext. 201 – Box Office
jamil@srtp.org
www.srtp.org
Artistic Director
Jamil Khoury
Managing Director
Josh Schultz
Executive Director
Malik Gillani
Budget
$279,000
Nearest Public Transit
Washington (Blue and Red Lines)

Send Headshots to
Jamil Khoury

> Silk Road Theatre Project showcases
> playwrights of Asian, Middle Eastern,
> and Mediterranean backgrounds whose
> works address themes relevant to the
> peoples of the Silk Road and their
> Diaspora communities. Pay is $800
> per production. Founded in 2002.

Soapbox Theatre Company
≣Sc **⟱D**

1824 Bridle Post Dr.
Aurora, IL 60506
630/728-0980
soapboxtheatre@yahoo.com
www.soapboxtheatre.com
Artistic Director
Nicole Warren
Managing Director
Christine Wortham
Send Headshots to
Christine Wortham

> Soapbox Theatre Company brings
> professional experiences to community
> theatre. No pay. Founded in 2006.

Speaking Ring Theatre Company
≣Sc **⟱D**

1733 W. Gregory St.
Chicago, IL 60640
312/458-9374
info@speakingringtheatre.org
www.speakingringtheatre.org
Artistic Director
Sean Leonard
Managing Director
John Henningsen
Budget
$20,000

> Speaking Ring Theatre gives voice to
> new ideas. Through new works and
> re-envisioned classics, this ensemble
> of artists tells stories that explore how
> far you are willing to go to fight for
> your beliefs. No pay. Founded in 2000.

Stage Left Theatre

▮E ▮Sy ▮D

3408 N. Sheffield Ave.
Chicago, IL 60657
773/883-8830
sltchicago@stagelefttheatre.com
www.stagelefttheatre.com
Producing Artistic Director
Kevin Heckman
Budget
$150,000
Nearest Public Transit
Belmont or Addison (Red Line)

> Stage Left produces and develops plays
> that raise debate on political and social
> issues. Pay is $200 per run. Founded in
> 1982.

Steep Theatre Company

▮E ▮Sc ▮D

3902 N. Sheridan Rd.
Chicago, IL 60613
312/458-0722
info@steeptheatre.com
www.steeptheatre.com
Executive Director
Peter Moore
Budget
$50,000
Nearest Public Transit
Sheridan (Red Line)
Send Headshots to
Julia Siple, Artist Liaison

> Steep Theatre is a company of artists
> who explore ensemble-based "Everyman"
> theatre. Founded in 2001.

Stockyards Theatre Project

▮Sy ▮D

6167 N. Broadway, #357
Chicago, IL 60626
773/936-7896
www.stockyardstheatreproject.org
Artistic Director
Artistic Council
Managing Director
Francesca Peppiatt
Budget
Under $10,000
Send Headshots to
Artistic Council

> Advancing women through theatre arts.
> No pay. Founded in 1999.

Strawdog Theatre Co.

▮E ▮Sc ▮D

3829 N. Broadway, 2nd Floor
Chicago, IL 60613
773/528-9889
773/528-9696 - Box Office
jaz@strawdog.org
www.strawdog.org
Artistic Director
Nic Dimond
Managing Director
Kyle Hillman
Budget
$150,000
Nearest Public Transit
Sheridan or Addison (Red Line)
Send Headshots to
Gregor Mortis, Casting Director

> From fresh takes on the classics and
> kitchen-sink dramas to inventive world
> premieres, Strawdog is committed to
> presenting great stories in their intimate
> black box theatre. No pay. Founded
> in 1987.

Studio Z

P.O. Box 577525
Chicago, IL 60657
312/543-7920
info@studioz.org
www.studioz.org
Artistic Director
Dan Zellner
Budget
$10,000
Send Headshots to
Dan Zellner

> Studio Z is dedicated to exploring the
> integration of digital multimedia and
> improvisation: exploring both a live
> multimedia stage and virtual environ-
> ments and using improvisation both for
> performance and authoring. Pay varies.
> Founded in 1992.

The Summer Place Theatre

P.O. Box 128
Naperville, IL 60566
630/416-3888
630/355-7969 - Box Office
info@summerplacetheatre.com
www.summerplacetheatre.com
Budget
$95,000

> Founded in 1966.

Sweat Girls Inc.

P. O. Box 180011
Chicago, IL 60618
dorothy@sweatgirls.org
www.sweatgirls.org

> Sweat Girls are a solo storytelling
> ensemble. Founded in 1993.

Teatro Luna

ⒶⒺ

5215 N. Ravenswood Ave.
Chicago, IL 60640
773/878-LUNA
teatroluna@aol.com
www.teatroluna.org
Budget
$80,000

> Dedicated to telling the stories of Latina
> women in an innovative way. Founded
> in 2000.

Theatre Building Chicago

ⒺSc **ⓓD**

1225 W. Belmont Ave.
Chicago, IL 60657
773/929-7367
773/327-5252 - Box Office
boxoffice@theatrebuildingchicago.org
www.theatrebuildingchicago.org
Artistic Director
John Sparks
Executive Director
Joan Mazzonelli
Budget
$1.4 million
Nearest Public Transit
Belmont (Brown, Red and
Purple Lines) or #77 bus
Send Headshots to
Allan Chambers, Assoc. Artistic Director

> Theatre Building Chicago is a rental
> house that provides subsidized spaces for
> theatre companies. They also help emerg-
> ing artists and companies. And they
> have a writers' workshop for the devel-
> opment of new musical theatre. Pay is
> $50 for readings, $750 for full presenta-
> tions. Founded in 1977. Theatre Building
> Chicago does use Equity actors under a
> Codes agreement for their annual Stages
> workshop.

Theatre Entropy

ⒺSc **ⓓD**

P.O. Box 577309
Chicago, IL 60657
773/505-6766
info@theatreentropy.org
www.theatreentropy.org
Artistic Director
Jon Arndt
Managing Director
Melissa Freiman
Budget
$15,000
Send Headshots to
Jon Arndt

> Theatre Entropy uses the stage as a
> catalyst for open discussion, provoking
> an examination of the existing social,
> cultural and political climate. No pay.
> Founded in 2003.

Theatres

Theatre Seven of Chicago

528 W. Wellington Ave.
Chicago, IL 60657
briang@theatresevenofchicago.org
www.theatresevenofchicago.org
Artistic Director
Brian Golden
Managing Director
Tracey Kaplan
Executive Director
Annie Erickson
Budget
$10,000
Send Headshots to
Tracey Kaplan

> With a critical respect for the written
> word, Theatre Seven creates a rich,
> vibrant work where many emotions,
> ideas, viewpoints and desires exist in
> contradiction. No pay. Founded in 2006.

Theatre-Hikes

4337 1/2 N. Richmond St., Apt. 2W
Chicago, IL 60618
773/293-1358
630/725-2066 - Box Office
theatrehikes@yahoo.com
www.theatre-hikes.org
Artistic Director
Frank Farrell
Budget
$40,000

> Theatre-Hikes takes an audience on a
> two mile hike presenting a complete
> play and performing the scenes from the
> play at different locations along the way.
> Pay is $20 a show. Founded in 2002.

Theo Ubique Theatre Company

1454 W. Fargo Ave., #3C
Chicago, IL 60626
773/370-0235
773/745-3355 - Box Office
www.theoubique.org
Co-Artistic Directors
Fred Anzevino
Beverle Bloch
Budget
$25,000
Nearest Public Transit
Morse (Red Line)
Send Headshots to
Fred Anzevino

> Theo Ubique presents intimate, minimalist
> musicals, revues, and plays in a cabaret
> theatre format. No pay. Founded in 1997.

Thunder & Lightning Ensemble

773/332-9939
info@thunderandlightning.org
www.thunderandlightning.org
Artistic Director
D.B. Schroeder,
Managing Director
Andrew Carl,
Budget
$30,000
Send Headshots to
D.B. Schroeder

> Thunder and Lightning attracts non-tra-
> ditional audiences by coupling unique
> outreach with all of their Main Stage
> productions. Pay is $100 per production.
> Founded in 2004.

Timber Lake Playhouse

8215 Black Oak Rd.
Mt. Carroll, IL 61053
815/244-2035
info@timberlakeplayhouse.org
www.timberlakeplayhouse.org
Artistic Director
Brad Lyons
Do not send headshots.

> Timber Lake is a summer stock theatre.
> Founded in 1961.

TimeLine Theatre Company

615 W. Wellington Ave.
Chicago, IL 60657
773/281-8463
773/281-8463 ext.24 - Box Office
info@timelinetheatre.com
www.timelinetheatre.com
Artistic Director
PJ Powers
Managing Director
Brian Voelker
Budget
$450,000
Nearest Public Transit
Wellington (Brown Line)
or Belmont (Red Line)
Send Headshots to
PJ Powers

> *TimeLine presents stories inspired by history that connect with today's social and political issues. Pay is $75 a week. Founded in 1997.*

Tinfish Productions
E **Sc**

4247 N. Lincoln Ave.
Chicago, IL 60618
847/392-0226 - Box Office
www.tinfish.org
Artistic Director
Dejan Avramovich

> *Tinfish's mission is to produce works by or about great European literary figures. Founded in 1994.*

TownSquare Players, Inc.
E **D**

121 E. Van Buren St.
Woodstock, IL 60098
312/985-4638
815/338-5300 - Box Office
Plockwoo@transunion.com
www.tspinc.org
Budget
$150,000
Send Headshots to
Paul Lockwood, Board Liaison

> *TownSquare Players, Inc. is a not-for-profit corporation established to provide local talent with theatrical opportunities. Founded in 1968.*

Trap Door Theatre
E **Sc** **D**

1655 W. Cortland Ave.
Chicago, IL 60622
773/384-0494
trap_door@earthlink.net
www.trapdoortheatre.com
Artistic Director
Beata Pilch
Executive Director
Nicole Weisner
Budget
$90,000
Nearest Public Transit
Damen (Blue Line)
Send Headshots to
Beata Pilch

> *Trap Door specializes in producing original or avant-garde European work that is rarely or never produced in the U.S. Pay is tips. Founded in 1994.*

Theatres

Uma Productions

P.O. Box 14416
Chicago, IL 60614-0416
773/347-1375
info@umaproductions.org
www.umaproductions.org
Artistic Director
Mikhael Garver
Managing Director
Jon Faris
Budget
$70,000
Send Headshots to
Audrey Francis, Casting Director

Village Players Theater

1010 Madison St.
Oak Park, IL 60302
708/524-1892
vptmanage@yahoo.com
www.village-players.org
Artistic Director
Carl Occhipinti
Managing Director
Scott Heckman
Executive Director
Bill Brennan
Budget
$250,000
Nearest Public Transit
Harlem (Green or Blue Lines)
Send Headshots to
Janet Louer
> *American Classics. Pay is $50 per production. Founded in 1960.*

Virtuoso Performing Arts

8321 W. Golf Rd.
Niles, IL 60714
847/583-0740
zizwiz@hotmail.com
www.virtuosoperformingarts.com
Artistic Director
David Zizic
Managing Director
Carrie Polack
Nearest Public Transit
Skokie (Yellow Line)
Send Headshots to
David Zizic
> *Young directors held to the highest standards of professionalism to create virtuoso performances. No pay. Founded in 2002.*

Vittum Theater

1012 N. Noble St.
Chicago, IL 60622
773/278-7471
773/342-4141 - Box Office
info@vittumtheater.org
www.vittumtheater.org
Artistic Director
Tom Arvetis
Managing Director
Scott Letscher
Budget
$60,000
Nearest Public Transit
Division (Blue Line)
Send Headshots to
Tom Arvetis
> *Vittum Theater presents Chicago's young audiences aged pre-teen through high school, educators and families with an affordable artistic experience rooted in performance. Pay varies. Founded in 1998.*

Vortex Theatre
☐D

1501 Barnsdale Rd.
LaGrange Park, IL 60526
708/354-4580
www.vortexlgp.org
Artistic Director
Gary Charles Metz
Budget
$8,000
Send Headshots to
Gary Charles Metz

> Vortex Theatre is a cutting-edge Park-
> District sponsored community theatre
> that produces original and lesser-known
> works, with occasional forays into the
> "mainstream." No pay. Founded in 1996.

Walkabout Theater
☐Sy

3241 N. Ravenswood Ave.
Chicago, IL 60657
773/248-9278
312/458-0566 - Box Office
kristan@walkabouttheater.org
www.walkabouttheater.org
Artistic Director
Kristan Schmidt
Managing Director
Karen Yates
Budget
$70,000
Send Headshots to
Kristan Schmidt

> Walkabout does new work in new
> ways, including site-specific locations.
> There is always pay, but it varies.
> Founded in 1999.

White Horse Theatre Company
☐Sc ☐D

1409 W. Farwell Ave., #3G
Chicago, IL 60626
773/272-5987
admin@whitehorsetheatre.com
www.whitehorsetheatre.com
Artistic Director
Jeremy Morton
Managing Director
Chad Weiden
Executive Director
Danny Sama
Budget
$60,000
Send Headshots to
Chad Weiden

> Reimagining musical theatre through
> intimate, yet innovative and creative
> productions. Pay is $250 per production.
> Founded in 2002.

WNEP Theater
☐Sy ☐D

2131 W. Cuyler Ave., #1
Chicago, IL 60618
info@wneptheater.org
www.wneptheater.org
Artistic Director
Jen Ellison
Send Headshots to
Jen Ellison

> WNEP cultivates original work that
> is critical of the American status quo,
> blurs the definitions of comedy and
> tragedy, and removes the line that
> separates spectator and participant.
> No pay. Founded in 1992.

Theatres

95

Wood Street Theater Company

P.O. Box 61
Palatine, IL 60078
847 / 358-6286
847 / 338-0706 - Box Office
WoodStTheater@aol.com
Artistic Director
Susannah Kist
Managing Director
Glen W. Jackson
Budget
$50,000
Send Headshots to
Susannah Kist

*Wood Street Theater is a community
theater that makes every effort to cast
all who audition, in combination with
more experienced actors. No pay.
Founded in 2002.*

Woodstock Musical Theatre Company

121 E. Van Buren St.
Woodstock, IL 60098
815 / 338-1789
815 / 338-5300 - Box Office
info@woodstocktheatre.com
www.woodstocktheatre.com
Budget
$150,000
Send Headshots to
Bob Riner, Board Liaison

*Not-for-profit corporation established
to provide local talent with theatrical
opportunities and to promote community theatre as an art form. No pay.
Founded in 1974.*

Young Actors Ensemble

5050 Church St.
Skokie, IL 60077
847 / 763-3514
847 / 763-3518 - Box Office
troth@gojcc.org
Artistic Director
Terri Hilton-Roth
Nearest Public Transit
Skokie (Yellow Line)

*The Young Actors Ensemble produces
high quality, family-oriented musicals
and dramas, typically with all-youth
casts and occassionally using actors of
all ages. No pay. Founded in 1996.*

4 Agents and
Casting Directors

How Do I Get an Agent?

BY CHRISTINA BIGGS

While it may not be mandatory to hire an agent, there are situations in Chicago where it may play to an actor's advantage. Agents act as the link between their clients and the producers, directors and casting directors looking to hire. And since agents make life so much easier for casters by filtering out unsuitable applicants, some casting directors will only work through agents.

"I'm hired by the production company or the studio and I rely on agents. When I'm told what the specs are, I call them to get suggestions for actors," says Claire Simon of Simon Casting. "We're out and we see shows and meet new talent, but we can't call everyone for every audition and we can't remember every fantastic talent." In fact, 90 percent of Simon Casting's projects deal only with actors with agents.

One of the actors' agent's main jobs is to raise awareness of their client and maximize the number of roles for which they might be considered. They are privy to information not available to the public—either directly from casters or through breakdown services, third party listing services that digitally link casting directors to agents.

"Part of my job is finding talent a job—through breakdown services, knowing the upcoming season at theatres and calling around. Just generally being in the pulse of what's going on locally," says Sam Samuelson of Stewart Talent.

The other important role of an agent is to negotiate contracts. An agent should be an expert on the gamut of options out there—LORT, CAT, Broadway and national tour, off-Broadway, TV, film, voice-over, radio. "All are union mandated templates but there are tons and tons of different contracts and every one has a different trick," says Samuelson. It's the union's job to track what an actor should be paid and the agent's job to make sure that money is received.

At a large company like Stewart, the majority of clients are union, but they will take on some young people who can be sent on both union and non-union jobs to build a resume. Also, there are available agents who work mainly with non-union actors, however those are fewer and the companies tend to be small. Incidentally, managers are allowed to negotiate a union contract but only if they are also a lawyer.

"If you're only interested in theatre, you might be able to do without an agent," says Simon. "For everything else, you definitely need one." So begin by looking into which agencies you'd like to approach. Ask fellow actors and directors or teachers for recommendations; check out agency Web sites; look to the list in this, as well as others, publications, such as ACT ONE REPORTS. Chicago agencies vary from large groups like Aria, Geddes and Stewart with maybe a dozen agents to smaller agencies like Talent Group, Inc, with just a few.

If you plan on sending a packet, do your homework first. Find a specific agent within the agency and create a presentation that is customized to what you've learned about that person. "To get hooked up with an agent, send a great picture; a short, concise letter—not funny—just, I'm new in town, I just did this show and here's my resume," says Simon. While black and white used to be the industry standard, the digital age is pushing the preference to color headshots.

Make sure that you respect their guidelines. Don't show up an hour earlier than the new talent call times expecting to make an impression by being singular. It will be the wrong impression. Don't solicit over the phone if they say no calls. Keep them updated on additional jobs you take but don't pester to the point of harassment.

There are also other ways that agents find talent in Chicago. "I see talent in shows and get recommendations from people we represent; recommendations from producers, directors, casting directors," says Samuelson. So send agents invitations to shows you'll be in, highlight reviews and mail them (they are a referral of a sort) and if you have a relationship with someone they represent, ask them to mention your name.

Once you have their attention, they may choose to represent you or to sign you. Unlike New York and L.A., Chicago actors are allowed to multi-list or be represented by more than one agent.

"Multi-list to start with, if you can," says Simon. "Establish good communication, get them interested and then go exclusive. The ultimate goal should be an exclusive relationship."

It should also be noted that multi-listing may not necessarily get you more work, since the majority of agents are working from the same lists. But it will allow you to test drive multiple personalities and figure out which relationship most suits your own personal tastes.

The way that agencies are structured is also different in Chicago. Film, TV, theatre, commercials and industrials are sometimes all handled by the same agent. In New York and L.A. they are very separate—the talent pool doesn't cross over. "We typically sign the ones who can do film, theatre and TV—strong in all the media forms," says Samuelson. "And if an agent wants to sign you, I'd sign." Signed actors can not multi-list, but they do get the added benefit of being pushed to the front of the line when it comes to selling them.

There should never be a fee for signing with an agency, but there will be commissions, whether represented or signed. Franchised or licensed agents enter into an agreement with all talent unions and the state under which they agree to abide by certain rules and conditions when dealing with performers who work within union jurisdiction. Once a represented or signed actor gets work, whether through their agent or on their own, they will pay their agent somewhere between 10 and 20 percent. Managers, who are not bound by union jurisdiction, can take between 5 and 25 percent, or whatever agreement they make with their client.

Once an actor lands an agent, the relationship that develops will be the key to their success. Constant communication is vital. The agent will present audition opportunities (how many depends on market conditions) and may also provide feedback from casting directors. Equally, an actor should keep notes about audition specifics and share that information with their agent.

"Check your messages all the time," says Samuelson. "I expect a call back as soon as possible." Simon says it's often the case for commercials that she'll get specs on a Tuesday, cast Wednesday and shoot on Thursday. Sometimes you won't hear from your agent for two or three weeks then they offer two auditions back to back. It's best always to be prepared.

Even if you're represented, that doesn't mean you should ever stop promoting yourself. "Just because you land an agent doesn't mean jobs will fall in your lap. But if two people are working on building a career that's better than one," says Samuelson. "We can't promise anything. We can only say we'll work on your behalf. An agent that can promise you work is predicting the future."

The Production Food Chain

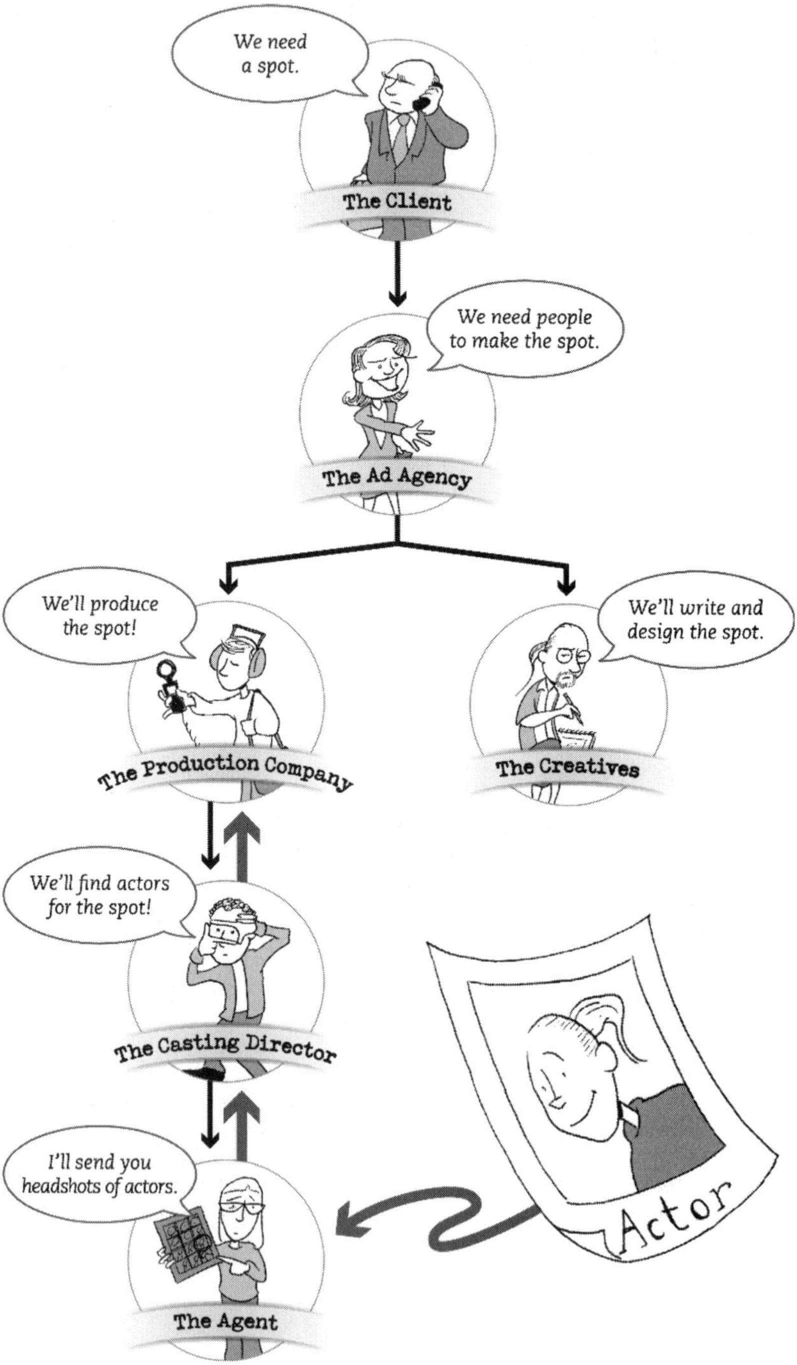

Understanding How You Get Paid (and Making Sure You Do)

BY BECKY BRETT

This how it works:

You get hired.

You do the shoot or voice-over.

The production company pays your agent.

Your agent pays you (and you pay your agent a percentage for his or her services).

This should happen in about 30 days.

Sometimes there are shorts in the system. The work gets done, then the production company takes a while to pay. Or the check comes and gets lost on the agent's desk.

Fortunately, actors have tools at the ready to help them get paid.

Union: The actors' unions require employers to post a bond. So, if the show closes early, or the production company skips town without paying, talent can still get something (though frequently not the entire amount owed).

Your union can also contact your agent and give them a friendly push to pay you—or to push the production company to cut the checks.

Non-Union: Getting paid by an unscrupulous employer or agent is a bit tougher if you're non-union. If you've contacted your agent and are getting the run-around, call the Illinois Department of Labor. Their number is 312/793-2808. And their Web site is *www.state.il.us/agency/idol*. There, you can download labor laws and complaint forms. Other states have departments of labor, too.

Here are some things you can do to ensure that you don't get into that situation:

Check references.

Ask your friends or colleagues what they think of the agents around town. Ask on the message boards on PERFORMINK's Web site.

Cultivate a good relationship with your agent.

Ultimately, communication is the key. The agent works for you, but it can sometimes feel like it's the other way around. Treat them with respect and they will do the same for you.

Read the fine print.

Read and understand your contract. Is there overtime pay? Is there a limit on the number of hours you can work in a day? Does it say when you'll get your check?

Here are some warning signs for situations to avoid:

- Your agent is also a casting director.

- An agent "discovers" you on the street or in a bar.

- They say they're a manager. (You generally don't need a manager in Chicago. When you need one, you'll be seasoned enough to know.)

- They don't seem to have an office.

- They require a "listing" fee from you.

- They push you to do something you're uncomfortable with.

- They won't tell you when you're being paid.

- The agent is not in this book or ACT ONE REPORTS.

Legal Resources

By Mechelle Moe

ften, actors are left to fend for themselves—particularly if they don't have union status. But never fear, there are a slew of government agencies set up to help you deal with disputes, claims and other legalities that may be out of your realm of knowledge. Below is a short list of key organizations you can contact for assistance.

EMPLOYMENT ISSUES

Illinois Department of Labor
160 N. LaSalle St., Suite C-1300
Chicago, IL 60601
312/793-2800
www.state.il.us/agency/idol

If you have a payment dispute with your employer, contact the Wage Claim Division of the Department of Labor. They'll step in if your employer has stiffed you on your wages. First, you'll need to file a complaint with the Wage Claim Division; next, they will send a letter to the employer on your behalf; after they have received a response, they will review the case and either dismiss the claim or move it to the next level—a hearing.

If the employer is found liable at the hearing, they are given a time period in which to make the payment. If they skip that, then the case is turned over to the Attorney General's office, where legal proceedings begin. It is important to stay in touch with the Department of Labor and keep them abreast of the situation and whether the claim has been resolved or not.

The Equal Employment Opportunity Commission

National Office
1801 L St. NW
Washington, DC 20507
202 / 663-4900
www.eeoc.gov

Chicago District Office
500 W. Madison St., Suite 2800
Chicago, IL 60661
312 / 353-2713

The EEOC protects individuals against discrimination—including race, color, sex, religion, national origin, age or disability—in the workplace, by a labor union or an employment agency when applying for a job. Charges may be filed through the EEOC office, but there are time restrictions. If you believe you were a victim of discrimination, act promptly.

In cases of sexual discrimination, women can contact the Women's Bureau (*www.dol.gov/wb/*). The bureau is not an enforcing agency. They focus on empowering women in the workplace, enhancing the work environment and providing a support network by providing resources and statistics.

Department of Human Rights

100 W. Randolph St., Suite 10-100
Chicago, IL 60601
312 / 814-6200
www.state.il.us/dhr/

The Department of Human Rights administers the Illinois Human Rights Act, which prohibits discrimination on the basis of race, color, religion, sex, national origin, ancestry, citizenship status (with regard to employment), age 40 and over, marital status, physical or mental handicap, military service or unfavorable military discharge. To initiate a charge, call, write or appear in person at the department's office within 180 days of the date the alleged discrimination took place. (Housing discrimination cases have a one-year filing deadline).

CONSUMER ISSUES

Office of Attorney General

Consumer Protection Bureau
500 S. 2nd St.
Springfield, IL 62706

Chicago Hotlines
800 / 386-5438
TTY 800 / 964-3013
www.ag.state.il.us

The Attorney General serves as the chief consumer protection official in Illinois, handling approximately 28,000 complaints annually. The Consumer Protection Bureau protects consumers and businesses who have been victimized by fraud, deception or unfair competition. Complaint forms can be downloaded from their Web site.

Better Business Bureau

BBB Chicago & N. Illinois
330 N. Wabash Ave., Suite 2006
Chicago, IL 60611
312 / 832-0500
feedback@chicago.bbb.org
www.chicago.bbb.org

The BBB handles anything that deals with contracts and obligations. They do not take sides in a dispute, but rather act as a mediator between the company and consumer to help both sides come to a resolution. Complaints the BBB tackles include misleading advertising, improper selling practices, non-delivery of goods or services, misrepresentation, unhonored guarantees or warranty, unsatisfactory service, credit/billing problems and unfulfilled contracts. They don't deal with discrimination or employment practices.

Talent Agencies - Union

Ambassador Talent
333 N. Michigan Ave., Suite 910
Chicago, IL 60601
312/641-3491

Send headshot and resume.
Agency will call, if interested.
All ages, 2 months and older.
SAG/AFTRA/AFM franchised.

Aria Talent Management
1017 W. Washington St., Suite 2C
Chicago, IL 60607
312/850-9671

Submit headshot and resume by mail.
Agency will contact you if interested.
No voice-over. Must be experienced
actors. Exclusive only. SASE if you
want pictures back
Robert Scroeder: *TV, Film, Theatre*
Daria Grubb: *TV, Film, Theatre*
Katherin E. Tenerowicz: *Commercial Print*
David Anderson: *Commercial Print*

Baker and Rowley
3106 S. Racine Ave.
Chicago, IL 60608
312/850-4700
www.bakerandrowleytalent.com
bandrtalent@comcast.net

Send five headshots/resumes and two
voice demos. Agents will contact you
if interested. Multi-cultural representa-
tion. AFTRA/SAG/Equity franchised.
Diane Rowley: *Director*

Big Mouth Talent
935 W. Chestnut St., Suite 415
Chicago, IL 60622
312/421-4400

Send headshot/resume with a SASE.
Agency will call if interested. All ages.
SAG/AFTRA/Equity franchised.
Brooke Tonneman

bmg Talent
456 N. May St.
Chicago, IL 60622
312/829-6361
www.bmgtalent.com

Send headshot/resume by mail
only. Agency will call if interested.
SAG/AFTRA/Equity franchised.
Greg Brown: *President*
Dawn Gavin: *Full-service Agent*

Encore Talent Agency, Inc.
1732 W. Hubbard St.
Chicago, IL 60622
312/738-0230

Send headshot/resume with a SASE. No
drop-ins. SAG/AFTRA/Equity franchised.
Susan Acuna
Dawn Gray

ETA Inc.
7558 S. South Chicago Ave.
Chicago, IL 60619-2644
773/752-3955
www.etacreativearts.org

Mail composites and resumes to Joan
P. Brown. Will contact you if interested.
SAG/AFTRA franchised.
Joan P. Brown: *Agent*

Geddes Agency
1633 N. Halsted St., Suite 300
Chicago, IL 60614
312/787-8333
www.geddes.net

Submit headshot/resume by mail
only. Agency will call if interested.
AFTRA/SAG/Equity franchised.
Elizabeth Geddes: *Vice President,*
Full-service Agent

Grossman and Jack

230 E. Ohio St., Suite 200
Chicago, IL 60611
312/587-1155
www.grossmanjack.com

Submit by mail. AFTRA/SAG/Equity franchised.

Linda Jack: *Voice-over*
Mickey Grossman: *On-camera*
Vanessa Lanier: *Voice-over*
Jenny Knuepfer: *On-camera*
Richard Shoff: *Voice-over*
Amie Richardson: *Children*
Nell Wasserstrom: *On-camera, Voice-over*

Shirley Hamilton, Inc.

333 E. Ontario St., Suite 302B
Chicago, IL 60611
312/787-4700
www.shirleyhamilton.com

Registration by mail only with SASE. Actors must submit headshot and resume. Agency will contact by mail, if interested. AFTRA/SAG/Equity franchised.

Shirley Hamilton: *President*
Lynne Hamilton: *Vice President*
Samm Mezak: *On-camera, Trade Show, Voice-over, TV, Film*
Briar Grant: *On-camera, Trade Show, Voice-over, TV, Film*
Laurie Hamilton: *Print, Marketing*

Innovative Artists Agency (Formerly, Voices Unlimted)

541 N. Fairbanks Ct., Suite 2735
Chicago, IL 60611
312/832-1113
www.voicesunlimited.com

Voice-over talent should submit by mail commercial and/or narrative tape, two minutes or less with resume. An agent will contact you if interested. Exclusive voice-over representation only. AFTRA/SAG franchised.

Linda Bracilano – *Voice-over*
Laurie Lambert – *Agent*
Sharon Wottrich – *Director*

Iris Talent

1932 S. Halsted St., 4th Floor
Chicago, IL 60608
312/563-1005

Submit headshot/resume by mail. Agency will contact you by phone if interested. AFTRA/SAG franchised.

Monica Campbell: *On-camera, Trade Show, TV, Runway, Commercial Print, Film*

Lily's Talent Agency, Inc.

1301 W. Washington St., Suite B
Chicago, IL 60607
312/601-2345

Submit two headshots and resumes and SASE by mail. Include phone number and statistics. Agency will respond if interested.

Lily Liu: *President*
Gina Stevanovich: *Voice-over, On-camera*
Andrea Shipp: *Print, Fashion, Voice-over, Theatre, Dance*

Naked Voices, Inc.

865 N. Sangamon St., Suite 415
Chicago, IL 60622
312/563-0136
www.nakedvoices.com

Submit a 2-minute, professionally made demo tape or CD by mail only.

Debby Kotzen: *Owner*

Salazar & Navas, Inc.

700 N. Green St., Suite 503
Chicago, IL 60622
312/666-1677

Hispanic/Latin types preferred, but all types considered and represented. Submit headshot/resume, and agency will respond if interested. AFTRA/SAG/Equity franchised.

Susana de Santigo: *President*
Martha Flores: *On-camera, Voice-over, Film, Commercial Print*

Norman Schucart Enterprises

1417 Green Bay Rd.
Highland Park, IL 60035
847/433-1113

Submit headshot/composite/resume with phone number by mail, with a SASE postcard. If interested, the agency will arrange to interview you in Chicago. AFTRA/SAG franchised.
Norman Schucart: *President, TV, Industrial Film, Print, Live Shows*
Nancy Elliot: *TV, Industrial Film, Print, Live Shows*

Stewart Talent

58 W. Huron St.
Chicago, IL 60610
312/943-3131
www.stewarttalent.com

Mail or drop-off (between 9-5, Mon-Fri) two headshots/resumes. The appropriate agent will contact you within six to eight weeks if interested. No walk-in interviews. No e-mails. AFTRA/SAG/Equity franchised.
Jane Stewart: *President*

Arlene Wilson Management

430 W. Erie St., #210
Chicago, IL 60610
312/573-0200

Submit headshot/resume by mail with SASE. The agency will contact you if interested. AFTRA/SAG/Equity franchised.
Erin Crews: *Agency Director, Commercial Print, Fashion Print*
Jessica Thomas: *Theatre, Film, TV*
Laura Alexander: *Children, On-camera, Commercial Print*
Erika Rohrich: *Children*
Jess Reuwer: *Commercial and Fashion Print*

Talent Agencies – Non-Union

Karen Stavins Enterprises, Inc.

303 E. Wacker Dr., Concourse Level
Chicago, IL 60601
312/938-1140
www.karenstavins.com

Submit headshot/resume, composites or voice tapes, attn: New Talent. Agency will contact you, if interested. Non-union talent booked for commercials, industrials, voice-over, trade shows, live shows and print. 17 years and older.

Nouvelle Talent

P.O. Box 578100
Chicago, IL 60657
312/944-1133

Send picture and resume. Agency will contact you if interested.
Ann Toni Sipka: *President, New York Trade Shows*
Carlotta Young: *Chicago Trade Shows*

Talent Group, Inc.

4755 N. Hermitage Ave.
Chicago, IL 60640
773/561-8814

No drop-ins. Send a headshot/resume or voice-over demo, attn: Karlie Sherman, New Talent. Ages 18 and older.
Karlie Sherman: *Agent*

Agents and Casting Directors

Talent Agencies – Milwaukee

Jennifer's Talent Unlimited, Inc.
740 N. Plankinton Ave., Suite 300
Milwaukee, WI 53203
414/277-9440
www.jenniferstalent.com
  Submit headshot/resume, and voice-over talent must submit CD. Attn: Marna Riordan. Agency will contact you if interested. SAG/AFTRA franchised.
  Jennifer L. Berg: President

Lori Lins, Ltd.
7611 W. Holmes Ave.
Milwaukee, WI 53220
414/282-3500
www.lorilins.com
  Submit headshot/resume and a cover letter. Agency will respond.
  Lori Lins: Owner
  Betty Antholine: Booking Agent

Arlene Wilson Talent, Inc.
807 N. Jefferson St., Suite 200
Milwaukee, WI 53202
414/283-5600
  Open call for actors Wed. 1:30-3:00 pm. Must have current headshot/resume and/or voice demo. May also send materials. SAG/AFTRA franchised.
  Carol Rathe: Voice-over, On-camera, Broadcast Director

Convention and Trade Show

Best Faces
1150 N. LaSalle St.
Chicago, IL 60610
312/944-3009
www.bestfacesofchicago.com
bestfaceschicago@aol.com
Send materials by mail, attn: Judy Mudd; agency will contact you if interested.

Corporate Presenters (A division of Karen Stavins Enterprises)
303 E. Wacker Dr., Concourse Level
Chicago, IL 60601
312/938-1140
www.corporatepresenters.com
Send composite, headshot or trade show demo, attn: New Talent. Agency will contact you if interested. Narrators, hosts/hostesses and models booked for trade shows, conventions, special promotions and variety acts. 17 years and older.

The Group, Ltd
3188 Castle Canyon Ave.
Henderson, NV 89052
702/895-8926
E-mail or mail materials (e-mail preferable; professional shots only). No drop-ins, and no talent under 20 years old. Trade show talent only. Interested in all talent including narration, foreign languages. Prefer audio prompter.
Bonnie Pattiz

Casting Directors

Jane Alderman Casting
640 N. LaSalle St., Suite 535
Chicago, IL 60610
312/397-1182
Do not call. Mail only.
Jane Alderman: *Casting Director*

Big House Casting & Audio
944 N. Noble St., #1
Chicago, IL 60622
773/772-9539
Send one demo/resume. Do not call.
Priscilla Quirino
Colleen Archer
Kate McClanaghan

Claire Simon Casting
1512 N. Fremont St., #202
Chicago, IL 60622
312/202-0124
Mail only.
Claire Simon

Ja-Sa-Rah Casting
700 N. Green St., Suite C20
Chicago, IL 60622
312/455-8383
jsarahcasting1@sbcglobal.net
Jacquelyn Conard

K.T.'s
773/525-1126

David O'Connor Casting
1017 W. Washington St., Suite 2A
Chicago, IL 60607
312/226-9112
David O'Connor

Segal Studio
1040 W. Huron St.
Chicago, IL 60622
312/563-9368
Jeffery Lyle Segal

Tenner Paskal and Rudnicke Casting
10 W. Hubbard St., Floor 2E, Suite 2N
Chicago, IL 60610
312/527-0665
www.tprcasting.com
Mickie Paskal: *Casting Director*
Jennifer Rudnicke: *Casting Director*

Trapdoor Casting
1655 W. Cortland St.
Chicago, IL 60622
773/384-0494
www.trapdoortheater.com
Beata Pilch
Nicole Wiesner

4 Agents and Casting Directors

5 On-Camera and
Voice-Over

It's a Living:
How Chicago Actors
Pay the Rent

By Becky Brett

I t is widely known that Chicago is a great theatre town for actors just starting out. Literally hundreds of theatre companies provide the space to hone your craft and experiment. But theatre in Chicago doesn't pay much, if at all. Even Equity actors aren't assured of making a living. And commercial and feature film work has slowed down considerably since the millennium.

Aside from getting a temp or restaurant job, how do Chicago actors make a living while staying in their field? We sat down with Anne Jacques, co-owner of Act One Studios, and talked about the usual suspects (industrials, print, etc.). We also uncovered some interesting and unusual ways actors in Chicago can cobble together a living that are less likely to involve the phrases, "How may I direct your call?" or, "Who's ready for dessert?"

Industrials: It used to be that industrial work was a Chicago actor's bread and butter. Jacques says, "In the 1980s and 90s an actor could count on multiple-day shoots using 10–15 actors." Industrials are training films for companies that teach things like customer service and how to use software, or informational pieces on social services, etc. As budgets got cut in the late 1990s, industrials shot for fewer days, using fewer actors, finally dissolving into often just a narrator/spokesperson.

Nothing fully filled the gap left by the industrials boom, but these can still be a significant source of income for actors because they look for a variety of types for them. One of the beauties of industrial film is that it can be a source of ongoing work. Jacques has worked with some clients for a decade or more. "If the client does a lot, they'll use you a lot once they've gotten to know you."

Two major types of actors can find work in industrials: the narrator/spokesperson and… well… everyone else.

The narrator/spokesperson is typically mainstream looking, attractive, wearing a suit and could believably be an executive or manager. Jacques notes that actors fitting this bill need a higher degree of specialized skills because they are most likely to be speaking lots of technical language and using an ear prompter. In her experience, "A client can't get a script fully written and approved by all the branches of their company in advance of the shoot, and they're plopping a 30–40 page script in your hands that morning." The actor then records him or herself reading the script, which is played back to them through the ear prompter.

Then there's "everyone else" in scene work in which you could be called upon to play anyone who works at a job or is a consumer, encompassing all types and ages. Your scenes could range from complex technical language to small everyday language, like how you would order something in a drugstore.

Extras: For the past several years there has been a new "extra" category for Chicago, which is SAG extra work. Any shoot on a SAG contract has to have a certain percentage of union extras. While a nonunion gig as an extra might pay $50–$75 for a day's work, which could be a 14-hour day, a union extra gets paid at a certain rate for a standard work day, which is eight out of nine hours. Working as a union extra, you get a meal break and an overtime rate if it goes past the eight hours of working.

Voice-over: Although many actors think of voice-over as a quick road to cash, Jacques recommends that voice-over should be the last thing you try to do because it requires some very refined skills. "When you're on stage, you have the physical components of the set and props, the duration over time, your fellow actors," she explains. "For voice-over you have to be good enough to craft that all up in your imagination instantaneously. It takes a great deal of experience." Also putting together a demo can become a large investment, not only of your money, but also the time that it takes to shop around. However, actors who do get in to voice-over can work a lot because their face doesn't become over used. The good ones know how to shave tenths of seconds off the air time and can bring nuances that beginners wouldn't even think of. Also, with the rise of the gaming industry, voice-over is gaining new forms beyond narration for commercials and radio spots.

Trade Shows: Chicago hosts many large conventions and trade shows throughout the year. Corporations often look for actors to use as narrators, hosts, and models for their displays and presentations. This can be pretty steady work and you may even get to travel. Check with your agent to see if they already have a trade show division.

Print: This is the kind of print work that is different from modeling and covers companies that want to include people of every demographic in their marketing campaigns—the "real people." Places you'll see this kind of work include the posters at your bank, brochures at the pharmacy and real estate ads in the newspaper. Even product packaging, such as toy boxes, might be a source of income. Check with your agent, or see the agent listings in this book, to see if they have a print department.

Other interesting sources of income: There is a company in Chicago called Law Actors, which provides actors to read depositions, participate in mock trials and present evidence at trial, among other things. Check out *www.lawactors.com* for more information.

Also, there are companies that hire actors for medical and corporate training exercises. Rush University Medical Center and UIC Medical Center are just a couple of teaching hospitals that utilize actors in their clinical training environments. Actors can check out *www.workplaceproductions.com* for corporate training gigs.

Finally, when all else fails, put on a costume and become a dancing banana. The Naked Juice Company recently held a promotion which included actors dressed up like fruit dancing all over Chicago. Apparently, it paid pretty well.

Following is a listing of production companies in Chicago. It's always smart to do a mailing to companies that do the work you're interested in getting hired for. Many actors find that companies will request them if they were really impressed with their tape or reel, or if they've worked with them before. If you've worked with a particular production company, remind them that you're still out there. If you haven't worked with a company, having your headshot, tape or reel in front of them will help them recognize you later when the casting director shows them the same stuff.

On-Camera and Voice-Over

Production Houses that Take Headshots

A&M Video Productions
Mark Hodges
2575 Waukegan Ave.
Highland Park, IL 60035
847 / 432-9306
www.anmvideo.com
anmvideo@gmail.com

ACA – Schuurman Communications
773 / 792-0241
www.schuurman.us
info@schuurman.us

Apache Films
Rich Trenbeth
773 / 262-7007

Bada Bing Productions
2313 W. North Ave.
Chicago, IL 60647
773 / 862-8717
www.badabingfilms.com
nick@badabingfilms.com

Bayly Regele
53 W. Jackson Blvd.
Chicago, IL 60604
312 / 939-3912

Big Shoulders Digital Productions
Production Manager
303 E. Wacker Dr., Suite 2000
Chicago, IL 60601
312 / 540-5400
www.bigshoulders.com
info@bigshoulders.com

Bitter Jester Productions
Nicolas Daniel
1907 Second St., Suite 2
Highland Park, IL 60035
847 / 433-8660
www.bitterjester.com
bje@bitterjester.com

Bodenworks
4755 N. Hermitage Ave.
Chicago, IL 60640
773 / 728-5800
www.bodenworks.com
bodenworks@aol.com

Brella Productions, Inc.
1601 Simpson St.
Evanston, IL 60201
847 / 864-4040
www.brella.com
sales@brella.com

Broadview Media, Inc.
Bonnie Hawksworth
Richard Hawksworth
142 E. Ontario St.
Chicago, IL 60611
312 / 337-6000
www.broadviewmedia.com
bonnieh@broadviewmedia.com

Byrne, Jennifer
2720 W. Cortland St.
Chicago, IL 60647

Close Encounter Productions
503 Crown Point Dr.
Buffalo Grove, IL 60089
847 / 215-3939

Cohen Communications Corp.
404 N. Grace St.
Lombard, IL 60148
630 / 627-6060

Communications Corporation of America
Fred Strauss
P.O. Box 14262
Chicago, IL 60614
773 / 348-0001

CVC Communications
165 N. Arlington Heights Rd.
Buffalo Grove, IL 60089
847 / 229-8333
www.cvccommunications.com

Ebel Productions, Inc.
340 N. Ogden Ave.
Chicago, IL 60607
312 / 222-1123

Filmontage Productions
Vladimir Vanmaule
9S150 Stearman Dr.
Naperville, IL 60564
630 / 904-4111
www.filmontage.com
filmontage@comcast.net

Fine Line Productions, Inc.
720 Telser Rd.
Lake Zurich, IL 60047
847 / 726-0066
www.finelineproductions.net
fineline4@mac.com

FrameOne, Inc.
1630 Payne St.
Evanston, IL 60201
847/332-2611
www.frameone.com
jbernin@frameone.com

Full Circle Creative Media Services, Inc.
Tami
4610 Main St.
Lisle, IL 60532
630/322-9327
www.fullcircle.bz
info@fullcircle.bz

Ron Gunther Productions
7631 Oriole Ave.
Niles, IL 60714
847/967-5933

HMS Media
110 S. River Rd.
Des Plaines, IL 60016
847/803-7000
www.hmsmedia.com

Infinite Video Productions
1880 E. Fabyan Pkwy.
Batavia, IL 60510
630/389-0000
www.infinitevideo.com
info@infinitevideo.com

Jacobsen Studios
1020 N. Western Ave.
Chicago, IL 60622
219/878-7200

Joe Blow Films
Julie Vargo & Associates
312/209-4848

Joyce Fox Productions, Inc.
Joyce Fox
2712 W. Greenleaf Ave.
Chicago, IL 60645
773/856-0388
www.joycefox.com
joyce@joycefox.com

Kandokid
Lauren McNamara
312/222-9335

Lewis Creative Radio, David
David Lewis
400 S. Green St.
Chicago, IL 60607
312/666-7911
drlewis@earthlink.net

Lichterman Productions, Inc.
737 N. May St.
Chicago, IL 60622
312/243-7788

Major Media Productions
P.O. Box 209
Deerfield, IL 60015
847/272-1400
www.major-media.com
joan@major-media.com

Mellenhead Productions
337 E. Maple Ave.
Mundelein, IL 60060
847/837-1886

Mimi Productions
112 S. Sangamon St., 3rd Floor
Chicago, IL 60607
312/829-0162
www.mimiproductions.com
info@mimiproductions.com

National Video-Documentors
2133 W. Wilson Ave.
Chicago, IL 60625
773/561-1646
www.nvd1.com

Newave Video Productions, Inc.
Steven Grein
9944 S. Roberts Rd., Suite 203
Palos Hills, IL 60465
708/598-6900
www.newavetv.com
steveg@NeWavetv.com

Orchard Productions
Katie Petrik
451 N. Racine Ave.
Chicago, IL 60622
312/421-9100
www.orchardpro.com
info@orchardpro.com

Papanek Film and Video
P.O. Box 319
Beverly Shores, IN 46301
219/872-6441
www.thompapanek.com
thomasp142@aol.com

Paul Fagan Productions
312/927-1001
pfagan@umich.edu

On-Camera and
Voice-Over

Pivotal Pictures
437 N. Wolcott Ave.
Chicago, IL 60622
312/226-9090
www.pivotalpictures.com
pivotal@pivotalpictures.com

Pixel Brothers, Inc.
1812 W. Hubbard St.
Chicago, IL 60622
312/733-7373
www.pixbros.com
info@pixbros.com

Pretty Boy Pictures
7051 S. Bennett Ave.
Chicago, IL 60649
773/858-6169
www.prettyboypicturesinc.com
kjoseph@prettyboypicturesinc.com

Ravenswood Media
4926 N. Wolcott Ave.
Chicago, IL 60640
773/271-0793
www.ravenswoodmedia.com

Red Eye Studio
2155 Stonington Ave.
Hoffman Estates, IL 60195
847/843-2438
www.redeye-studio.com

Richter Brothers Studio
Sarah Mueller
921 W. Van Buren St., #240
Chicago, IL 60607
312/861-9999
www.richterbrothers.com
info@richterbrothers.com

Mark Schimmel Productions
818 Pinto Ln.
Northbrook, IL 60062
847/400-5145
www.markschimmel.com

Spi-TV Media Group
A Silhouette Productions, Inc. Company
3711 N. Ravenswood Ave., Suite 109
Chicago, IL 60613
773/525-5546
www.spi-tv.com
info@spi-tv.com

Spot the Monkey
David Wittenstein
222 W. Ontario St., Suite 501
Chicago, IL 60610
312/867-0707
www.spotthemonkey.com
davidwittensteinadigitalvision@ameritech.net

Stage Fright Productions
David Phyfer
P.O. Box 373
Geneva, IL 60134
800/979-6800
www.stagefrightproductions.com
david@stagefrightproductions.com

T.M. Productions
34 Steeplechase Dr.
Hawthorn Woods, IL 60047
847/937-0238

Tall Tree Productions, Ltd.
Bruce Razniewski
2037 Central Ave.
Wilmette, IL 60091
847/853-9322
www.talltree.tv
bruce@talltree.tv

Tango Films Incorporated
Robert Yeomans
1423 Elmwood Ave.
Evanston, IL 60201
847/905-1240
www.tangofilmschicago.com
robert@tangofilmschicago.com

Tri-Marq Communications
25 S. Washington St., Suite 212
Naperville, IL 60540
630/961-1575
www.trimarq.com
mail@trimarq.com

Twitch Films, Inc.
1930 W. Wellington Ave.
Chicago, IL 60657
773/929-3629
www.twitchfilms.tv
info@twitchfilms.tv

Walking Shadows Productions, Inc.
401 W. Ontario St., Suite 205
Chicago, IL 60610
312/274-9850
www.walkingshadowsproductions.com
info@walkingshadowsproductions.com

Wedgeworth Business Communications, Inc.
807 Madison St., Suite 111
Oak Park, IL 60302
708/445-8585
www.wedgeworthbiz.com
pamela@wedgeworthbiz.com

Demo Tapes & CDs

Audio Producers Group
Mindy Verson
300 N. State St., Suite 3206
Chicago, IL 60610
312/220-5423
mindy@audioproducersgroup.com

BAM Studios
Dave Leffel
One E. Erie St., Suite 350
Chicago, IL 60611
312/255-8862
www.bamstudio.com
dave@bamstudio.com

Bobby Schiff Music Productions
363 Longcommon Rd.
Riverside, IL 60546
708/442-3168
www.bobbyschiffmusic.com
bobby@bobbyschiffmusic.com

Bosco Productions
160 E. Grand Ave., 6th Flr.
Chicago, IL 60611
312/644-8300
www.boscoproductions.com

Rainbow Bridge Recording
117 W. Rockland Rd.
Libertyville, IL 60048
847/362-4060
www.rbrproductions.com

On-Camera and Voice-Over

Sound Advice
944 N. Noble St. #1
Chicago, IL 60622
773/772-9539
www.voiceoverinfo.com
info@voiceoverdemos.com

> *How do you succeed in voiceover and*
> *commercial acting? Learn from the best*
> *in the business at Sound Advice. We've*
> *produced more than 3,000 demos to*
> *date and trained nearly 9,000 working*
> *talent. Our success rate is unparalleled-*
> *anywhere! Visit www.voiceoverinfo.com,*
> *then call 773/772-9539*
> **See our ad on page 121.**

Sound/Video Impressions
110 S. River Rd.
Des Plaines, IL 60016
847/297-4360

Transalarm Recordings
2121 Dewey Ave., Suite D
Evanston, IL 60201
800/381-0841
www.taraudio.com
contact@taraudio.com
See our ad on page 122.

Wide Screen Films
Richard Diaz
773/841-3456
www.performancereels.com
widescreenfilms@aol.com

Reels

Absolute Video Services, Inc.
715 S. Euclid Ave.
Oak Park, IL 60302
708/386-7550

Allied Vaughn
1200 E. Thorndale Ave.
Elk Grove Village, IL 60007
847/595-2900
www.alliedvaughn.com

Atomic Imaging, Inc.
1501 N. Magnolia Ave.
Chicago, IL 60622
312/649-1800
www.atomicimaging.com

Broadview Media
142 E. Ontario St.
Chicago, IL 60611
312/337-6000
www.broadviewmedia.com

ELB's Entertainment, Inc.
2501 N. Lincoln Ave., Suite 198
Chicago, IL 60614
800/656-4585
www.elbsentertainment.com

Nxtrm (Pronounced Nextroom)
230 E. Ontario St., Suite 302
Chicago, IL 60611
312/335-3620

Video Replay, Inc.
118 W. Grand Ave.
Chicago, IL 60610
312/467-0425
www.videoreplaychicago.com

6 Unions and
Organizations

Actors' Equity Association

BY CARRIE L. KAUFMAN

Unions and
Organization

n a summer, 2006, gathering of actors in Chicago, a bunch of people decided to calculate if an Equity actor could actually make a living just on stage without having to tour outside of the Chicagoland area. Calculations were made based on the top Chicago Area Theatre (CAT) contract, Tier 6, which pays $686.25 a week, not including overtime, to an actor. Rehearsal times and runs of shows vary, but let's just say that a lucky actor actually works all 52 weeks a year. He earns a whopping salary of $35,685, without having to teach or wait tables or do voice or on-camera work.

But how many actors work 52 weeks a year?

To be sure, it's possible. Broadway and touring shows, which includes the Chicago sit-down production of Wicked, pay actors a minimum of $1,465 per week, plus a $113 per diem for traveling. And touring productions do often run 52 weeks a year, earning actors a pretty tidy sum.

And an actor who works close to all year usually has agreements with the theatres he works for that pay him over Equity minimum. So an actor might do, say, four shows a year and take home about $30,000.

But when was the last time you were cast in four Equity shows? And $30,000 is hardly enough to live on in Chicago.

"I don't think you possibly can make a living [on stage]," said Mary Ann Thebus, who is one of the most prolific actors in Chicago. "Maybe if you work at the main-stage at the Goodman all the time, maybe you can eke out some sort of a living, but most people don't do that."

So, why go Equity? That's a tough question, and almost all theatre professionals in Chicago are in agreement that a young actor just starting out should not try to get into the union. The aim is to get cast in as many shows as possible, get lots of experience and become a better actor. We have 50 Equity theatres listed in this book, and 15 of those are only Tier N or Tier 1—meaning the theatre only has to hire one Equity actor. In contrast, we have 150 non-Equity theatres listed. And there are often roles for non-Equity actors in Equity theatres.

But at some point, you'll want to consider joining the union. You get older and realize that if you're going to work a day job and do theatre, you really should get paid for the theatre work; and that whittling down the amount of work isn't a bad trade-off. Or you start getting some on-camera work or teaching and find that getting paid for theatre would actually mean you could give up your non-acting day job. Or you start getting cast regularly at one of the main Equity theatres in town. Or you want to go to New York, where it is always advantageous to arrive with an Equity card.

Another reason to turn Equity is that you get health and pension benefits. To qualify for six months of health insurance, you must work at least 12 weeks on an Equity contract—even a CAT N or CAT 1 contract—within a given 12 months. To get a year's worth of health insurance, you must work 20 weeks in 12 months CAT N theatres do not have to pay health insurance the first year they sign with Equity. Health insurance payments from CAT N theatres start in the theatre's second year of the contract.

For pension, most theatres pay the equivalent of 8 percent of an actor's gross weekly salary to the pension fund. That money can add up over the years, providing you with a nice retirement or supplemental income as you get older.

Contracts

If and when you do decide to go Equity, there are three ways to get into the union. One is to belong to one of the sister unions: The American Federation of Television and Radio Artists (AFTRA), The Screen Actors Guild (SAG), The American Guild of Musical Artists (AGMA) or The American Guild of Variety Artists (AGVA). Simply show them your membership card for those unions, fill out the application and pay the fees, and you're in Actors' Equity.

Another way is to simply get cast in an Equity role. It happens, especially in Chicago, where non-Equity actors are often seen by casting directors from Equity theatres.

A third way is to join the Equity Membership Candidate program. The EMC program simply allows you to earn a point every week you work in an Equity theatre on a non-Equity role. Once you get 50 points, then the union asks that the next Equity theatre that hires you puts you on an Equity contract.

If you are hired under an Equity contract, you should expect to work the Chicago Area Theatre (CAT) contract, as that's the most common. There are seven tiers to the CAT contract, starting at Tier N and ending at Tier 6, where we started this article.

Here is a breakdown of the weekly gross pay for cat contracts:

Tier	Actor Pay	SM Pay	Max Number Performances/Week	Insurance Contribution by the Theatre
N	$161.50	not required	1ST two years	$113.75*
1	$162.50	$201.50	4	$113.75
2	$233.00	$268.75	5	$113.75
3	$319.75	$371.50	6	$116.75
4	$465.25	$534.00	7	$122.75
5	$572.00	$669.25	8	$134.75
6	$686.25	$820.75	8	$144.75

after first year

The Goodman, Northlight and Court theatres are under LORT contracts, as they belong to the League of Resident Theatres that negotiates with Equity nationally. The Albert Theatre at the Goodman is a LORT B+. The Goodman Owen, Northlight and Court theatres are LORT D.

Here is a breakdown of the gross pay for lort:

Category	Actor Pay	SM Pay	Ins. Contribution
A	$816.00	$1,181.00	$142.00
B+	$769.00	$1,020.00	$142.00
B	$714.00	$851.00	$142.00
C	$663.00	$794.00	$142.00
D	$536.00	$661.00	$142.00
Experimental	$427.00	$488.00	$142.00

Marriott's Theatre in Lincolnshire, Drury Lane Oakbrook and Second City are all on Special Agreements negotiated directly with Actors' Equity Central Region. (Drury Lane Water Tower is on a CAT contract.) Equity Central Region also administers the Second City Detroit and Las Vegas contracts.

Marriott actors make $611 per week (going up to $623 on May 23, 2007) and stage managers make $887 (going up to $905). Drury Lane Oakbrook actors make $593 (going up to $605 in May) and stage managers make $862 (going to $879).

Second City mainstage actors make $647 for eight shows a week (going up in April to $669) while stage managers get $771 (going to $798). Second City etc. actors get $485 a week for six shows (going up to $501 in April) while stage managers get $578 (going to $598).

You can also work at Marriott's, Drury Lane Oakbrook, Chicago Shakespeare and Chicago Children's Theatre under the Theatre for Young Audiences (TYA) contract.

Here is the gross pay for tya:

Category	Actor Pay	SM Pay	Actor/SM	Ins. Contribution
Weekly Tier I	$407.00	$541.00	$426.00	$140.00
Weekly Tier II*	$407.00	$570.00	$456.00	$140.00
Per Performance I	$82.00	$103.00	$95.00	n/a
Per Performance II	$65.00	$88.00	$70.00	n/a

for touring companies

Fees

Joining Actors' Equity will cost $1,100 in initiation fees, but actors and stage managers have two years to pay it. You get full member benefits after paying only $400 of the initiation fee. But you lose all money paid if you fail to pay the entire $1,100 within two years.

Equity has two yearly dues structures. Members must pay base dues of $118 a year, billed at $59 each May and November. In addition, actors and stage managers pay 2.25 percent of their gross earnings, up to $300,000. So what you pay depends on how much you work.

That's about it. Actors' Equity has a pretty comprehensive and easy to use Web site. Go to *www.actorsequity.org* for more information. And, good luck with your decision.

Unions and Organization

AFTRA/SAG

BY CARRIE L. KAUFMAN

he Screen Actors Guild (SAG) and the American Federation of Television and Radio Artists (AFTRA) are the unions in which most actors make their money. They cover radio, television and film. And, while there is some non-union work in Chicago most of the on-camera or voice-over work here is union.

In Chicago, the path to joining AFTRA or SAG is through actual work. Get an agent. Get your agent to send you out for jobs. Land a job. If you start landing union jobs, then you join the union.

In general SAG is the contract used for a theatrical film, whether that film will ever actually make it to theatres or not. A TV Movie of the Week is usually SAG, as are most independent films—the ones that decide to work with union actors.

AFTRA covers variety TV, which used to mean the "Carol Burnett Show" but today can cover a lot of reality television, such as "American Idol."

AFTRA also covers radio, recordings, industrials, daytime talk shows and soap operas, and newscasters, among others.

Commercials can be both AFTRA and SAG, and it's an area that the two unions continuously argue about. Historically, it has depended on the medium on which the commercial is shot. Film is SAG. Video is AFTRA. But what categorydoes digital fall into? Even many theatrical films aren't shot on film anymore. In Chicago, the general rule is that the commercial shoot is whichever union the producer chooses.

Chicago can do that because AFTRA and SAG are administered from the same regional office. In L.A. and New York, they have separate offices with separate staffs.

Joining

Becoming a member of AFTRA is pretty easy. You don't have to pre-qualify. You don't have to get a job. You don't have to prove you're a professional actor or newscaster or recording artist. You just have to have the $1,363.90 initiation fee, and be willing to pay dues, which are based on a percentage of your earnings. But before you pay that kind of money, it's wise to be sure you're going to earn it back with AFTRA work.

For SAG, there are a few more hoops to jump through before you get the privilege of paying them your $1,658 initiation fee and dues. You have to get a SAG job in order to be eligible to join the union. In Chicago, this is possible, as agents will send out non-SAG actors to SAG auditions. In Los Angeles, you can't get an agent without your SAG card. It's sort of a vicious circle. That's something to keep in mind if you're thinking about heading west.

And if you do get a union job, you don't have to join SAG or AFTRA right away. The Taft-Hartley Act (or the National Labor Relations Act) provides that an employee must have 30 days before being required to join the union. That gives a steelworker a month to see if he likes the job before ponying up his fees and dues. But actors can work one day, then not get another union job for months, or years. Or, an actor can get cast in something that will give him a week's worth of work, then he might catch a break and get a day job two weeks later. He can work all of those jobs without having to join the union. But the first job he gets after 30 days from his first day of employment, he must join the union.

This can be something of a financial strain, since you could very well be paying more to join the union than you get paid in the 30 days after you've landed your first job. Session fees for commercials, for instance, currently run at $567.10 for on-camera and $426.39 for voice-over. Then you get paid a fee for the actual run of the commercial—either a 13-week lump sum fee or a residual every time it runs. But those fees aren't always paid in a timely manner. And you could be faced with landing a second SAG job outside of the initial 30-day period, before you have been paid the equivalent of the initiation fee from your first SAG job.

Benefits

Pension and health plans are part of SAG and AFTRA, just as they are part of any union. Each job an actor works, the producer is required to pay into the pension and health plans. And actors are also required to pay for part of their health coverage.

In the age of skyrocketing health care costs, the bar has risen steeply to be covered by a union plan. For SAG, actors must make a minimum of $13,790 in a 12-month period to qualify for the union's stripped-down health insurance plan. For the better plan, actors must earn at least $28,120. The bar is lowered for actors over 40, who have qualified for health coverage for at least 10 years during their careers. They are eligible for further coverage if they earn $10,000 in a year.

For AFTRA, actors must earn at least $10,000 to be eligible for an individual health plan. For a family plan, an actor has to earn at least $30,000 on an AFTRA contract.

Other benefits to joining a union are that they negotiate work rules and ensure that you don't get ripped off or taken advantage of. If you're on a shoot and something comes up that is questionable (you're asked to skip a meal or work overtime without being paid overtime rates), then tell the production manager that it's all right with you if it's all right with your agent and union, then give one of them a call. Don't argue with the production manager yourself. Let them go to bat for you. That's one of the benefits of being in a union.

Unions and Organization

Unions

Actors' Equity Association
125 S. Clark St., Suite 1500
Chicago, IL 60603
312/641-0393
Audition Phone: 312/641-0418
www.actorsequity.org

American Federation of Television and Radio Artists (AFTRA)
1 E. Erie St., Suite 650
Chicago, IL 60611
312/573-8081
www.aftra.org

American Guild of Musical Artists
1430 Broadway, 14th Floor
New York, NY 10018
212/265-3687
agma@musicalartist.org
www.musicalartist.org
Barbara Hillman, Midwest
Representative
bhillman@cornfieldandfeldman.com
312/236-7800

American Guild of Variety Artists
184 Fifth Ave., 6TH Floor
New York, NY 10010
212/675-1003

Directors Guild of America
Chicago Headquarters
400 N. Michigan Ave., Suite 307
Chicago, IL 60611
312/644-5050
800/599-1675
www.dga.org

Screen Actors Guild
Chicago Regional Office
1 E. Erie St., Suite 650
Chicago, IL 60611
312/573-8081
www.sag.org

Helpful Organizations

The Actors' Fund
Don Towne, LCSW
203 N. Wabash Ave., Suite 2104
Chicago, IL 60610
312/372-0989
www.actorsfund.org
dtowne@actorsfund.org

Arts and Business Council of Chicago
70 E. Lake St., Suite 500
Chicago, IL 60601
312/372-1876
www.artsbiz-chicago.org
info@artsbiz-chicago.com

Association of Consultants to Nonprofits
216 W. Jackson Blvd., Suite 625
Chicago, IL 60606
312/580-1875
www.acnconsult.org
info@acnconsult.org

Chicago Department of Cultural Affairs
312/742-1175
www.ci.chi.il.us/culturalaffairs

Community Media Workshop at Columbia College
600 S. Michigan Ave.
Chicago, IL 60605
312/344-6400
www.newstips.org
cmw@newstips.org

CPAs for Public Interest
550 W. Jackson Blvd., Suite 900
Chicago, IL 60661
312/993-0407
www.cpaspi.org

Chicago Department of Revenue
312/747-3823
www.ci.chi.il.us/revenue

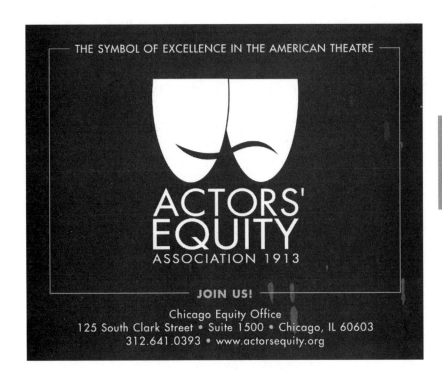

Unions and Organization

Donors Forum of Chicago
208 S. LaSalle St., Suite 740
Chicago, IL 60604
312/578-0175
www.donorsforum.org
info@donorsforum.org

Executive Service Corps of Chicago
25 E. Washington St., Suite 1500
Chicago, IL 60602
312/580-1840
www.esc-chicago.org

Illinois Arts Alliance
203 N. Wabash Ave., Suite 1920
Chicago, IL 60601
312/855-3105
www.artsalliance.org
info@artsalliance.org

Illinois Arts Council
100 W. Randolph St., Suite 10-500
Chicago, IL 60601
800/237-6994
www.state.il.us/agency/iac
info@arts.state.il.us

League of Chicago Theatres
228 S. Wabash Ave., Suite 200
Chicago, IL 60604
312/554-9800
www.chicagoplays.com
info@chicagoplays.com

National Dinner Theatre Association
David Czarnecki
www.ndta.com

Nonprofit Financial Center
29 E. Madison St. Suite 1005
Chicago, IL 60602
312/376-7962
www.nonprofitfinancial.org

**The Saints (Volunteers
for Performing Arts)**
Athanaeum Theatre
2936 N. Southport Ave., Rm. 203
Chicago, IL 60657
773/529-5510
www.saintschicago.org
office@saintschicago.org

Season of Concern
Stephen Rader
203 N. Wabash Ave., Suite 2104
Chicago, IL 60601
312/332-0518
www.seasonofconcern.org

**Society of Stage Directors and
Choreographers (SSDC)**
1501 Broadway, Suite 1701
New York, NY 10036
212/391-1070
www.ssdc.org

Breadth of Training

By Jenn Q. Goddu

hen you look at it, when you really look at it, you'll find the breadth of performer training in Chicago is astounding. Acting? Scene study? Commercial auditioning? Digital filmmaking? Playwriting? Sound or lighting design? On-camera work? Improv? Circus arts? Kids classes? You can find all of these in and around Chicago.

Yes, you may have gone to a conservatory, but if you want to work in a city as competitive as Chicago, you need to keep your skills current. Taking additional classes can have extra benefits such as networking. Translation: You can meet people who might get you cast. And, besides, taking action to further your training is better than sitting at home feeling sorry for yourself if an audition doesn't go your way.

Here's a round-up of classes offered in the city to help you sort out where to start your self-improvement or skills-enhancement regime.

Acting/Performance

"One of the things that has changed in the Chicago market over the past 10 or 15 years is that the acting population has doubled, if not tripled," said Steve Merle at **Act One Studios.** "It used to be that you could get by without taking classes. I don't think that's true anymore."

He recommends actors make classes part of their routine when they're not in a show. Keep working your skills to stay competitive, "or you're not going to survive in this market. The level of Chicago talent is getting awfully good," he said.

With some 35 different classes offered at all levels, Act One considers itself a "full-service acting training center." Teachers working in the industry lead classes typically capped at 10 students. The school's goal is "to create a supportive atmosphere and give people tools that they can go out and use."

Training

Act One doesn't have the market cornered on supportive learning environments, however. **The Actors Workshop** has been working since 1991 to teach primarily Stanislavsky systems in a welcoming environment. The ideal student, said artistic director Michael Colucci, is someone who sees ongoing learning as a foundation of their craft.

Another long-time acting school in the city is **Acting Studio Chicago** (formerly the Audition Studio). Its training is based upon 12 guideposts outlined by casting director Michael Shurtleff. This is, according to center director Rachael Patterson, an "incredibly practical approach to script analysis that leads the actor to personalization and action."

On the south side, **eta Creative Arts Foundation** offers acting classes for kids and adults, but the company has also branched out into lighting (beginning and advanced classes), sound and playwriting.

Another of the city's Meisner-oriented schools is **The Artistic Home** which teaches performers to work "moment to moment" in technique and scene study classes. There is also an Audition Intensive.

Speaking of intensive, another program that allows actors to hone their skills is **The School at Steppenwolf**. Founded in 1998, this is a training residency for professional actors incorporating Viewpoints, Meisner, Improvisation and Feldenkrais into scene study.

Victory Gardens opens its theatres to its training program so its beginning, intermediate, advanced and master acting class participants can play out their scenes on stage rather than in a classroom or studio space. The theatre also offers voice and physical technique classes as well as workshops such as "Making A Living in the Arts" or "Writing with Actors." (There's a writing section below, but note that Victory Gardens also offers Playwriting and Directing classes.)

Dawn Arnold teaches **Moving Dock Theatre Company's** classes in Michael Chekhov's Acting Technique. "The technique has within it fantastic possibilities for actors," she said. "It's designed to keep awakening more of an actor's potential. So I think an actor could come to a Chekhov and always move forward."

"Personalized attention" is also the aim of **Chicago Actors Studio**. It offers workshops in Stanislavsky and Meisner methods taught at beginning, intermediate and advanced levels that students can transition in and out of as they are ready, said director Edward Dennis Fogel.

In the suburbs there are more theatres with class offerings for kids and adults.

The best known is probably the **Piven Theatre Workshop** in Evanston. The curriculum has expanded over the past 30 years, but the bulk of the training is based in theatre games and improvisation, inspired by a number of teachers, including Viola Spolin and Uta Hagen. "Our program honestly suits everyone," said artistic director Jennifer Green. "No matter what someone wants from the experience, we have something really cool within the community to offer them."

Apple Tree's **Eileen Boevers Performing Arts Workshop**, up in Highland Park, gets 'em started young, offering year-round classes in theatre performance for children as young as four.

In the south suburbs, Etel Billig teaches kids and adults at the **Illinois Theatre Center**. Her philosophy is to get students to appreciate theatre from the actors point of view. Alumni include Michael Shannon, who appeared on ITC's stage when he was 16. Billig was named "Best Muse for Children" in Chicago Magazine's "Best of Chicago" issue in 2004.

The **Village Players Theatre in Oak Park** runs the gamut with its classes. One season's offerings included Digital Filmmaking for Young Adults, The Opera Workshop, storytelling, scene study classes and courses based on Julia Cameron's book *The Artist's Way* or aimed at helping performers lose their inhibitions.

Sarantos Studios is also located in Oak Park. Ted Sarantos brings 35 years of teaching experience to his classes for professional and non-professional actors.

Most of these training programs have some sort of performance built into the training, although students do, at times, have to reach advanced levels before they will get to take the stage in front of an audience.

One more performance-focused program is the **Neo-Futurists**, offering workshops focusing on the principles of Neo-Futurism, taught by creator Greg Allen. But they also have a more theoretical class looking at the Historical Inspirations of Neo-Futurism such as Italian Futurism, Dadaism, Surrealism, Jerry Grotowski, Fluxus and Augusto Boal.

This approach is not so much acting but rather, as the course descriptions suggest, learning "how to be yourself on stage" while "creating an engaging, artistic response to your life and your immediate surroundings."

Film

The **Chicago Filmmakers Co-op** teaches film production, screenwriting, digital moviemaking, editing on Final Cut Pro and lighting for film and video in college-level classes taught by industry professionals. To make it easier for people to learn new skills while maintaining a day job, the classes are offered weeknights and weekends.

In addition, **Women in Film Chicago** offers The Build-A-Skill Series, providing a forum where women can gain real-world knowledge to utilize in their day-to-day career pursuits within the industry.

Improv

Of course Chicago is a great town in which to learn improvisation skills. We have a number of theatres offering different approaches to the form.

At **Annoyance**, classes of 16 or fewer students focus on the individual as an improviser. The philosophy, according to managing director Mike Canale, is "the best thing you can do for your scene partner is go out with a strong emotion, a strong character, something strong."

I.O.'s Training Center, on the other hand, works to build a sense of ensemble among students while teaching the long-form structure developed by Del Close.

"The form of the Harold produces a very well-rounded improviser," said training center director Rachel Mason. Classes train people to "follow their fear" and enjoy the adventure. "Here we are, seven people training together becoming like a tribe, trying to fight the universe and produce art."

ComedySportz's six levels of training teach short-form game-based improvisation. Also part of their core curriculum is a course on how to use genre in improvisation, and a class on musical improv.

The Playground Theater offers performance workshops to give performers a chance to learn and perform, and a Master's Series for more advanced improvisers from around the city.

For people in the northern suburbs or southern Wisconsin, there's **Improv Playhouse,** which also teaches acting. Located in Libertyville, they have intro and professional level classes for adults and kids.

7 Training

Of course the big name in improv training is **The Second City Training Center** which has 1,300 to 2,000 students registered at any given time.

"We are very much about strong scenes that have strong relationships, environment and point of view and structures to them," said Rob Chambers, president of Second City Training Centers & Education Programs.

Second City's introductory improvisation course is the most popular; classes of eight to 16 people are taught skills they can apply on stage and off, such as listening, team building, ability to work in ensemble, problem solving, self confidence and even empathy.

Second City also offers classes in acting, directing, writing and musical theatre.

"People think of us as improv and comedy and we really have a whole lot more," Chambers said.

Movement

The Actors Gymnasium is the place to learn the highly athletic discipline of circus arts. The 11-year-old school, affiliated with Lookingglass Theatre, teaches juggling and gymnastics as well as offering voice and body strength development classes, stage combat and dialects for the stage.

But the most popular class at this circus and performing arts school is the Introduction to Circus Arts. Adults and youths can enroll in classes, whatever their previous experience. "I have a lot of people who call and they are very unsure. They say, 'I really haven't done anything,' and I assure them, 'That's just fine,'" said managing director Jennifer Jolls.

Another place to learn movement is **Plasticene**, one of the city's experimental theatre companies. In intensive workshops, the theatre emphasizes acting and theatre founded in the body, space and objects. The aim is to build physical control and spatial awareness through yoga, corporal mime, Boal, Grotowski, Zaporah, and contact improvisation.

On-Camera

Many of the acting training programs listed above offer on-camera classes, but other schools make preparing for commercial, television and film work their primary focus.

Sean Bradley and David Murphy at **The Green Room: An Actors' Studio** focus on on-camera acting in commercial audition, TV and film intensives and cold reading and monologue classes. "We bring all of our teaching directly from having run thousands of casting sessions," Bradley said. "We teach specific skills and how they apply to an audition."

The **Performance Learning Center** offers classes in commercial and ear prompter technique as well as scene study and monologue. Its "Getting Started" series is aimed at helping actors and models evaluate their talent and learn to market their potential and drive their own careers.

Another school with a career-building focus is **TVI Actors Studio**, with its courses in acting for theatre, but also film, TV and commercial techniques. An outpost of an L.A.-based company, the studios also offer day courses in sitcoms, voice-overs and preparing for prime time TV.

"It's really letting the actor realize that there is an actual business side to acting," said TVI consultant Veronica Simms. "As much as this is a creative lifestyle...you've got to know certain things if you do want to get ahead and make some money at it."

Shakespeare

The **Chicago Shakespeare Theater** actually got its start in the early 1980s as a training program with artistic director Barbara Gaines teaching Shakespeare Folio Technique in a rented hall in Wrigleyville. Now the company is established in a swank space on Navy Pier, but teaching of Folio Technique continues.

The company's Classical Training Project features monologue, scene study and acting with stage combat for classes of 8 to 12 students.

The Folio Technique class isn't billed as an acting class, but rather an opportunity to better understand Shakespeare and how he meant his works to be performed. Using the original Folio texts, the class introduces students to verse speaking and clues the Bard left in the text. "We are teaching you how to act Shakespeare, not read it the way you learned it in a classroom," said project administrator Reetu Gowdar.

[Editor's Note: There are other Shakespeare classes that arise from time to time, or that come in from New York or London. Only Chicago-based programs are the focus of this article.]

Writing

The mission of **Chicago Dramatists** is to develop new works and new playwrights, said Russ Tutterow. To that end, it regularly organizes intensive writing workshops in addition to offering a range of classes for playwrights at all levels of progress.

"There's always a playwriting fundamentals class that anyone can take, even if they haven't written a play," Tutterow said. But resident dramatists also teach courses in revising work or developing solo projects. Other guest instructors are invited to speak about dramaturgy as well.

Aspiring composers, lyricists and book writers should look at **Theatre Building Chicago's Writers' Workshop**. The program is dedicated to developing and producing new musicals.

The **Chicago Alliance for Playwrights** also sometimes does workshops.

In addition to these classes, there are myriad coaches on the Chicago scene, who teach anything from singing to voice-over to dialects and monologues. Peruse the following listings. You can train for years in Chicago and never get enough.

The
Conservatory
at Act One Studios

Two Years
that will
Change Your Life

Classes - Acting

Act One Studios, Inc.

640 N. LaSalle St., Suite 535
Chicago, IL 60610
312/787-9384
www.actone.com

Commercial Technique I
Get "camera-ready" for all types
of commercial auditions.

Industrial Film & Ear Prompter
Learn to analyze and perform technical
scripts and use ear prompter.

TV & Film I, II & Workshop
Learn the "ins and outs" of the
film and television world.

**Fundementals I, II & Scene
& Monologue Workshop**
Learn to make effective choices
from the script.

Acting Instinctively
Flexibility, creativity, and imaginative
freedom are explored.

Meisner Technique I, II & Workshop
Leads to a very truthful moment-
to-moment style of acting.

Audition Technique I & II
Learn the art of cold reading
theatre auditions.

Shakespeare Beg. & Adv.
Approaches based on the work
of Shakespeare & Co.

Masters Class
An ongoing scene study class
taught by Steve Scott.

Voice-Over I &II
Learn what it takes to be successful
in the voice-over market.

Movement Scene Study
Learn to bring a physical
life to your character.

See our ad on page 142.

Acting Studio Chicago

Rachael Patterson
10 W. Hubbard St., Suite 2E
Chicago, IL 60610
312/527-4566
www.actingstudiochicago.com
info@actingstudiochicago.com

Acting Studio Chicago is committed to
training actors in a challenging, supportive and professional environment.
We take special care to place students
in classes that are commensurate with
their level of skill and to keep class
sizes small. Our teaching is based upon
the 12 Guideposts of Michael Shurtleff,
author of "Audition." This technique
offers a path of creative discovery
through action. Est. 1981.
Classes offered include:

Core Program Levels 1-3
Start your training here!

On-Camera Classes
Strengthen your skills for commercial,
film and television.

Cold Reading
Learn to make strong, personal choices
quickly and "on your feet."

Monologue
Students work on 3 individually
assigned pieces from classical to
contemporary.

Advanced Scene Study
Scenes are assigned on a prescriptive
basis and actors are pushed past their
self-imposed boundaries.

Masters Scene Study
8 Chicago directors in 8 weeks.

Voice-Over Class
Learn all aspects of the Voice-Over
Business.

Weekend Workshops
A variety of offerings including classes
taught by top chicago casting directors
and directors.

See our ad on page 144.

7 Training

Actors Workshop Theatre

Michael Colucci
1044 W. Bryn Mawr Ave.
Chicago, IL 60660
312/622-1136
www.actorsworkshop.org
colucci@actorsworkshop.org

> Unlimited classes for a flat fee of
> $125 per month, including Scene Study,
> Meisner, Monologue, and Commercial. We
> offer a professional training program for
> all levels from beginner to professional.
> Visitors are always welcome.
> 773/728-PLAY or
> www.actorsworkshop.org.
> **See our ad on page 144.**

The Artistic Home

1420 W. Irving Park Rd.
Chicago, IL 60613
773/404-1100
www.theartistichome.org
info@theartistichome.org

> Technique 1, 2, 3
> Scene Study
> Acting for Film 1 and 2
> Voice for the Actor
> Playwrights Up and Moving
> The Artistic Home's curriculum is a
> Meisner-based technique augmented by
> L.A. and Chicago working experience
> that emphasizes living moment to
> moment, making strong choices and
> developing emotional freedom. Play-
> wrights and directors are offered hands-
> on experience in scene study, showcases
> and workshops of new scripts.
> Instructors: Kathy Scambiatterra, John
> Mossman, Mary Ann Thebus, CeCe
> Klinger, Patrick Thornton, Gillian Kelly.

Bob Bills Studio

Bob Bills
650 W. Lake St., Suite 410
Chicago, IL 60661
312/928-0638
www.bobbillsstudio.com
bb@bobbillsacting.com

> At Bob Bills Studio, we specialize in
> helping you breathe life into your craft.
> The art of acting comes when you apply
> your unique self to the framework that
> craft & technique help you build. Bob
> Bills Studio is at the intersection of the
> art & craft of acting.

Chicago Actors Studio

2040 N. Elston Ave.
Chicago, IL 60614
773/645-0222
www.actors-studio.net
chiactorsstudio@aol.com

> Centrally located in Chicago with classes
> for beginners to working professionals.
> A training faculty with over 60 years of
> combined experience that understands
> each student's individualized needs, cre-
> ating supportive and encouraging envi-
> ronments. Classes include scene study,
> character development, film, commer-
> cials, stage, voice/diction, auditioning,
> marketing, student showcase produc-
> tions, etc. The school has its own theatre,
> TV station and boot camp.
> **See our ad on page 146.**

Chicago Center for the Performing Arts Training Center

777 N. Green St.
Chicago, IL 60622
312/733-6714
www.theaterland.com
boxoffice@theaterland.com

eta Creative Arts

Abena Joan Brown
7558 S. S. Chicago Ave.
Chicago, IL 60619
773/752-3955
www.etacreativearts.org
email@etacreativearts.org

> Adult Acting – Beginning and
>   Advanced
> Sound, Lighting, Stage
>   Management, Playwriting
> How to audition for commercials

The Green Room
Sean Bradley
1915 W. Chicago Ave., #1
Chicago, IL 60622
312/421-2774
info@thegreenroomstudio.tv
5-Level On-Camera Training Program
Scene Study with Steven Ivcich
TV Auditions and Pilot Season
Intro to On-Camera
On-Camera Intensive I & II
Energy and Creativity
Personal Coaching
See our ad on page 148.

Illinois Theare Center
Etel Billig
P.O. Box 397
Park Forest, IL 60466
708/481-3510
www.ilthctr.org
ilthctr@sbcglobal.net
ITC offers classes for children (7 yrs. and older), teens and adults (beginning and advanced levels), and private coaching for auditions and college theatre

programs. All courses offer instruction in movement, voice and diction, character development, scene study, improv, and use of the imagination. Fall, Winter, Spring (10-week sessions).

The Neo-Futurists
Sharon Greene
5153 N. Ashland Ave.
Chicago, IL 60640
773/878-4557
www.neofuturists.org
info@neofuturists.org
The Neo-Futurists Performance Workshop and advanced Neo-Futurist Performance Workshop – Both workshops focus on introducing students to a new non-illusory method of writing, directing, and performing original work using their own lives and immediate environment.

Ask your agent where to go for On-Camera Training.

The Green Room was created by Sean Bradley and David Murphy, and built upon years of experience as Casting Directors working on thousands of on-camera projects. We teach the styles that are current today. We teach old dogs new tricks. We teach differently than anyone else.
And we repeatedly hear:
"I learned more in the first day than I have in all the other classes I've taken in town combined."

ADULTS - TEENS - KIDS

312-421-2774
www.thegreenroomstudio.tv

Performance Learning Center

Brian Boden
4755 N. Hermitage Ave.
Chicago, IL 60640
773/728-5800
www.plcchicago.com
brian@plcchicago.com

Piccolo Theatre

John Szostek
600 Main St.
Evanston, IL 60202
847/424-0089
www.piccolo.com
school@piccolotheatre.com

Piven Theatre Workshop

Jennifer Sultz
927 Noyes St.
Evanston, IL 60201
847/866-6597
www.piventheatre.org
jsultz@piventheatre.org

This renowned training center offers beginning, intermediate and professional level classes in improvisation, theatre games, story theatre, and scene study. Submit H/R for intermediate and advanced scene study. Come learn to play again at the theatre school that launched John & Joan Cusack, Aiden Quinn, Lili Taylor, Jeremy Piven and many more! Classes for young people from 4th grade through high school. Call for current class information.
See our ad on page 147.

Sarantos Studios

Ted Sarantos
405 South Blvd.
Oak Park, IL 60302
708/848-1100
www.sarantosstudios.com
info@sarantosstudios.com

Feature Film Acting
Scene Study
Monologue Preparation
On-Camera Auditioning
Basic Acting Technique
All students have the opportunity to have their best videotaped scenes and film footage posted at no charge on our Web

site for viewing by any casting directors. For examples, go to:
www.sarantosstudios.com/bm

The School at Steppenwolf

758 W. North Ave., 4th Flr.
Chicago, IL 60610
312/335-1888 ext. 5608
www.steppenwolf.org
info@steppenwolf.org

Founded in 1998, The School at Steppenwolf immerses gifted actors in the ensemble traditions, values and methods that make Steppenwolf unique. Our previous faculty and staff have been unanimous in praise of the environment that the School creates for actors to practice the craft they love as they learn more about the power of working together.

The Studio of The Moving Dock Theatre Company

Dawn Arnold, Artistic Director
410 S. Michigan Ave., Suite 720
Chicago, IL 60605
312/427-5490
www.movingdock.org
contact@movingdock.org

The Studio of The Moving Dock Theatre Company specializes in the Michael Chekhov Acting Technique, a dynamic acting approach that combines physical expressiveness with authentic psychological connection. An excellent approach for many styles of performing, our workshops offer a valuable resource to pre-professional and professional level actors who want to constantly take their acting to the next level. Introductory and continuing workshops are offered regularly in both eight-week and Weekend Intensive formats. Ongoing Company Class is offered for advanced students of the Chekhov Technique.
See our ad on page 150.

Training

"All true artists, especially the talented creators for the stage, bear within themselves a deeply rooted and often unconscious desire for transformation."

—Michael Chekhov

HUNGRY...to explore?
to discover?
to go beyond?

Be the Actor You Desire to Be.

Our workshops in the **Michael Chekhov Acting Technique** offer you a way to continue to develop your acting art. Each workshop engages you with the essentials of acting:

- The Actor's Way of Knowing—the actor's body, presence and expression
- Developing the Imagination
- Elements of Character
- Desire and Fulfillment—Relationship and Action—inner and outer dramatic action

Create your own combination of workshops from:

- **Weekend Intensives**—appropriate for newcomers and continuing students
- **Weekly Workshops**—to give you a way to keep connected to your acting.

Watch **movingdock.org** for all our exciting upcoming workshops and projects in the Studio!

The Studio of The Moving Dock
410 S. Michigan Ave. | Suite 720 | Chicago IL 60605
312.427.5490 | movingdock.org

The Training Center at Victory Gardens Greenhouse

2257 N. Lincoln Ave.
Chicago, IL 60614
773/549-5788
www.victorygardens.org
information@victorygardens.org

> The Training Center maintains that in the realm of theatre training there is no one particular approach that will work for all people. With the diversity of our instructors, who are working professionals, and a variety of class offerings for beginners to professionals, VGT is confident that students can find a class to both challenge and inspire. William Petersen, of "CSI" fame and former VGT student, believes, "Victory Gardens is the most important theatre in America. Through helping develop plays and playwrights, young actors and designers almost exclusively, the Gardens has literally grown and stocked American Theatre for over 30 years." Classes are offered in acting fundamentals, scene study, monologues, dialects, audition, Meisner, Alexander Technique, Feldenkrais, ALBA, among many others. Visit the Web site for current class schedule.

TUTA Theatre Lab

2032 W. Fulton St., Suite F-263-A
Chicago, IL 60612
847/217-0691
www.tutato.com
> Body, Object, and Space
> Master Class: The New Monologue
> Master Class: Chekhov

TVI Studios

116 W. Illinois St., Suite 3E
Chicago, IL 60610
312/828-0053, 800/884-2772, ext. 3
www.tvistudios.com
> Agent Evaluation Series
> Cold Reading
> Commercial
> Scene Study
> Auditioning for Theatre

Classes – Dance

American Dance Center Ballet Co.

10464 W. 163rd Pl.
Orland Park, IL 60467
708/747-4969
www.americandancecenter.com
> Ballet, Point, Jazz, Hip-Hop, Modern, Tap, Swing

Ballet Chicago

Jennifer Colgan
218 S. Wabash Ave., 3rd Flr.
Chicago, IL 60604
312/251-8838
www.balletchicago.org
info@balletchicago.org
> Ballet (ages 2 1/2-adult); Prepatory, Student, Professional Training, and Open/Adult Fitness divisions; Arts industry class card discounts available

Training

Beverly Arts Center
Erin Ryan
2407 W. 111th St.
Chicago, IL 60655
773/445-3838
www.beverlyartscenter.org
info@beverlyartscenter.org
*Ballet, Jazz, Modern, Tap, Stretch
and Strength, African*

Boitsov Classical Ballet
410 S. Michigan Ave. , Suite 300
Chicago, IL 60605
312/663-0844
www.boitsovballet.com
*Ballet – Vaganova Technique (Moscow
Bolshoi Theatre system of training)*

Chicago Multicultural Dance Center
806 S. Plymouth Ct.
Chicago, IL 60605
312/461-0030
www.cmdschool.com
Ballet, Jazz, Tap, Latin, Modern, Hip-Hop

**Chicago National Association
of Dance Masters**
5411 E. State St., Suite 202
Rockford, IL 61108
815/397-6052
www.cnadm.com
cnadm@megsinet.com
Workshops only; no ongoing classes

Dance Center Evanston
1934 Dempster St.
Evanston, IL 60202
847/328-6683
www.dancecenterevanston.com
dce@dancecenerevanston.com
Ballet, Jazz, Tap, Ballroom, Modern

Dance Dimensions
595B N. Pinecrest Rd.
Bollingbrook, IL 60440
630/739-1195
www.dancedimentionsstudio.com
*Ballet, Jazz, Tap, Ballroom, Swing,
Tumbling, Salsa*

Dance Therapy Center
Fine Arts Building
410 S. Michigan Ave.
Chicago, IL 60605
312/461-9826
Ballet, Modern, Dance Therapy

Dancecenter North
540 N. Milwaukee Ave.
Libertyville, IL 60048
847/367-7970
www.dancenter-north.com
info@dancenter-north.com
*Classical Ballet, Point, Jazz, Tap,
Irish Step Dance, Social Dance,
Jazz, Funk, Pilates and Extensive
Pre-School Program*

Discovery Center
2940 N. Lincoln Ave.
Chicago, IL 60657
773/348-8120
www.discoverycenter.cc
dcenter@core.com
*Ballet, Jazz, Modern, Tap, Ballroom,
Belly Dance, Contemporary Latin, Hip-
Hop, Salsa, Social Dance, Swing, Tango,
Kardio Kickboxing*

**Evanston School of Ballet
Foundation**
Kerry Hubata
1933 Central St.
Evanston, IL 60201
847/475-9225
Classical Ballet

Gus Giordano Dance Center
614 Davis St.
Evanston, IL 60201
847/866-9442
www.giordanodancecenter.com
info@giordanodancecenter.com
*Ballet, Jazz, Modern, Tap, Hip-Hop,
Ballroom, Pilates, Children's programs*

Hedwig Dances
Administrative Offices
2936 N. Southport Ave., Suite 210
Chicago, IL 60657
773/871-0872
www.hedwigdances.com
*Modern, African, Yoga, Hip-Hop, Tai
Chi, Company Class, Beginning Ballet,
Children's Classes*

Joel Hall Dance Center

1511 W. Berwyn Ave.
Chicago, IL 60640
773/293-0900
www.joelhall.org
joelhall@hotmail.com
Ballet, Jazz, Modern, Tap, Hip-Hop,
Egyptian, Pilates

Lou Conte Dance Studio

1147 W. Jackson Blvd. Walker
Chicago, IL 60607
312/850-9766
www.hubbardstreetdance.com
Home of Hubbard St. Dance Chicago.
Ballet, Jazz, Modern, Tap, Dance Fitness,
Hip-Hop, African

Muntu Dance Theatre of Chicago

6800 S. Wentworth Ave., Suite 3E96
Chicago, IL 60621
773/602-1135
www.muntu.com
info@muntu.com
African and African-American Dance,
Music and Folklore

North Shore School of Dance

505 Laurel Ave.
Highland Park, IL 60035
847/432-2060
www.northshoredance.com
Ballet, Jazz, Modern, Tap, Hip-Hop,
Irish, Yoga

Old Town School of Folk Music

4544 N. Lincoln Ave.
Chicago, IL 60625
773/728-6000
www.oldtownschool.org
Ballet, Jazz, Tap, African, Aztec, Belly,
Breakdance, Flamenco, Flat-Foot, Hip-
Hop, Hula, Indian, Irish, Latin, Mexican,
Swing, Tango, Brazillian, Capoeira

Rockford Dance Company

711 N. Main St.
Rockford, IL 61103
815/963-3341
www.rockforddancecompany.com
Ballet, Jazz, Modern, Tap, Ballroom,
Tango Argentino, Irish Folk

Ruth Page School of Dance

1016 N. Dearborn St.
Chicago, IL 60610
312/337-6543
www.ruthpage.org
Ballet, Jazz, Tap, Pilates

School of Performing Arts

200 E. 5th Ave., Suite 132
Naperville, IL 60563
630/717-6622
www.schoolofperformingarts.com
Ballet, Jazz, Modern, Tap, Hip-Hop, Fine
Arts Adventures (Preschool)

Shelley's School of Dance and Modeling, Ltd.

450 Peterson Rd.
Libertyville, IL 60048
847/816-1711
Ballet, Jazz, Modern, Tap, Hip-Hop,
Lyrical, Point

Teresa Cullen

721 Lake Ave., Suite 5A
Wilmette, IL 60091
847/832-0584
Flamenco, Ballet

The Academy of Dance Arts

1524 Centre Circle Dr.
Downers Grove, IL 60515
630/495-4940
www.theacademy-ibt.com
academyibtinfo@sbcglobal.net
Pre-Dance (ages 2 1/2-5),
Pre-Ballet (ages 5-6),
Ballet (ages 6 – Pre-Professional),
Pointe, Tap & Jazz (ages 5 – adult),
Hip-Hop (ages 8 – adult), Modern
(ages 13 & up), Lyrical (ages 12 & up).

2 Training

Classes - Filmmaking

Chicago Filmmakers Co-op
5243 N. Clark St.
Chicago, IL 60640
773 / 293-1447
www.chicagofilmmakers.org
    Film Production 1
    Digital Moviemaking
    Screenwriting 1
    Screenwriting 2
    Final Cut Pro
    Intermediate Final Cut Pro
    Directing
    Lighting for Film and Video

Columbia College
600 S. Michigan Ave.
Chicago, IL 60605
312 / 344-6101
www.colum.edu
etmazzocco@colum.edu
    MFAs offered in 10 disciplines focusing
    on the arts, media, education, and com-
    munication.

School of the Art Institute
36 S. Wabash Ave.
Chicago, IL 60603
312 / 345-3538
www.artic.edu
admiss@artic.edu
    MFAs offered in Performance,
    Film, Video and New Media.

Classes - Improv

Annoyance Theatre
4840 N. Broadway
Chicago, IL 60640
773 / 561-4665
www.theannoyance.com

ComedySportz
David Montgomery
3220 N. Lincoln Ave.
Chicago, IL 60657
773 / 549-8080
www.comedysportzchicago.com
davidmontgomery@comedysportzchicago.com
    See our ad on page 155.

The Improv Playhouse
David Stuart
116 Lake St.
Libertyville, IL 60048
847 / 968-4529
www.improvplayhouse.com
info@improvplayhouse.com
    Improv Playhouse is a comprehensive,
    professional actor training organization
    that offers classes and instruction for
    youth and adults, corporate training
    and development, and event planning
    and entertainment. They also produce
    traditional theatre and improv comedy
    performances.
    See our ad on page 154.

7 Training 2

153

iO (formerly ImprovOlympic)
3541 N. Clark St.
Chicago, IL 60657
773/880-0199
www.iochicago.net

Old Town School of Folk Music
4544 N. Lincoln Ave.
Chicago, IL 60625
773/728-6000
www.oldtownschool.org

Piccolo Theatre
John Szostek
600 Main St.
Evanston, IL 60202
847/424-0089
www.piccolo.com
school@piccolotheatre.com

The Playground
3209 N. Halsted St.
Chicago, IL 60657
773/871-3793
www.the-playground.com
info@the-playground.com

The Second City
1616 N. Wells St.
Chicago, IL 60614
312/664-3959
www.secondcity.com
sc1616@secondcity.com
See our ad on page 155.

Classes - Kids

About Face Youth Theatre
Paula Gilovich
1222 W. Wilson Ave., 2nd Flr. West
Chicago, IL 60640
773/784-8565
www.aboutfaceyouththeatre.com
paula@aboutfacetheatre.com

This six-month performance workshop explores storytelling, interviewing and performance techniques, as well as lectures and discussion with artists, activists and community leaders. The workshop culminates in a five-week run of a newly developed play.

Act One Studios, Inc.
Steve Merle
640 N. LaSalle St., Suite 535
Chicago, IL 60610
312/787-9384
www.actone.com
info@actone.com

Beginninig and advanced on-camera classes meet for nine weeks.
See our ad on page 142.

Acting Studio Chicago
Rachael Patterson
10 W. Hubbard St., Suite 2E
Chicago, IL 60610
312/527-4566
www.actingstudiochicago.com
info@actingstudiochicago.com
Classes and Workshops including:
Auditioning for Film/TV, Auditioning
for Commercials, Auditioning for Theatre,
Boot Camp, Monologue, Week Long
Summer Programs. We specialize in
bridging the gap between the industry's
needs and young actors' abilities.
See our ad on page 144.

The Actors Gymnasium
Nathan Drackett
Noyes Cultural Arts Center
927 Noyes St.
Evanston, IL 60201
847/328-2795
www.actorsgymnasium.com
info@actorsgymnasium.com
Offers a variety of physical theatre and
circus arts classes. Offers a variety of
movement classes based on gymnastics,
tumbling and dance for kids and parents.
See our ad on page 156.

Beverly Arts Center
Erin Ryan
2407 W. 111th St.
Chicago, IL 60643
773/445-3838
www.beverlyartscenter.org
info@beverlyartscenter.org
Four week dance camp combines
creative movement and pre-ballet
games and exercises.

Chicago Center for the Performing Arts Training Center
Siobhan Sullivan
777 N. Green St.
Chicago, IL 60622
312/327-2040
www.theaterland.com/training.htm
Offers a variety of classes for teenaged
actors, including acting for stage and
screen, improv, musical and on-camera
technique.

Chicago Filmmakers Co-op
5243 N. Clark St.
Chicago, IL 60640
773/293-1447
www.chicagofilmmakers.org
Digital moviemaking summer camp
for kids and teens.

Chicago Moving Company
3035 N. Hoyne Ave., 2nd Flr.
Chicago, IL 60618
773/880-5402
www.chicagomovingcompany.org
Offers a creative movement class avail-
able through the "Arts Partners in
Residence" program with the Chicago
Park District. For ages 10 and up, they
offer modern dance, drumming and
visual arts. It's free through the Chicago
Park District.

DePaul University School of Music
Community Music Division
Susanne Baker
804 W. Beldon Ave., Suite 328
Chicago, IL 60614
773/325-7262
www.music.depaul.edu/cmd
communitymusic@depaul.edu
The Musical Theatre Workshop for
Teens focuses on acting, movement
and vocal technique.

Eileen Boevers Performing Arts Workshop
Goose Haile
1850 Green Bay Rd., Suite 100
Highland Park, IL 60035
847/432-8223
www.appletreetheatre.com
rhaile@appletreetheatre.com
Acting, singing and dancing classes.

eta Creative Arts
Abena Joan Brown
7558 S. South Chicago Ave.
Chicago, IL 60619
773/752-3955
www.etacreativearts.org
email@etacreativearts.org
September through June, eta offers classes
focusing on drama, music and dance.

7 Training

Free Street

Bryn Magnus
1419 W. Blackhawk St.
Chicago, IL 60622
773/772-7248
www.freestreet.org
gogogo@freestreet.org

> *Pang is Free St.'s teen company, which produces performance exchanges with other visionary artists. Teenstreet is a multi-tiered jobs program designed to perform free shows for children throughout the city. Teenstreet offers a summer-only component of their performance jobs for teens program.*

Gallery 37 Center for the Arts

66 E. Randolph St.
Chicago, IL 60601
312/744-9249
www.gallery37.org
info@gallery37.org

> *This eight-week summer training course provides apprentice artists an opportunity to work with professional artists in theatre, music, writing and visual arts.*

The Green Room

Sean Bradley
1915 W. Chicago Ave., #1
Chicago, IL 60622
312/421-2774
info@thegreenroomstudio.tv

> *Kids On-Camera (5-7, 8-10, 11-13)*
> *Teens On-Camera (14-18)*
> **See our ad on page 148.**

Illinois Theatre Center

Etel Billig
P.O. Box 397
Park Forest, IL 60466
708/481-3510
www.ilthctr.org
ilthctr@sbcglobal.net

> *The theatre offers a summer arts day camp that encompasses music, dance, creative writing, theatre and art.*

The Improv Playhouse

David Stuart
116 Lake St.
Libertyville, IL 60048
847/968-4529
www.improvplayhouse.com
info@improvplayhouse.com

> *Offers a variety of improv and performing arts classes for young performers, including theatre games, musical theatre, voice and creative drama.*
> **See our ad on page 154.**

Lookingglass

Nina O'Keefe
2936 N. Southport Ave., 3rd Flr.
Chicago, IL 60657
773/477-9257 ext. 193
www.lookingglasstheatre.org
nokeefe@lookingglasstheatre.org

> *Lookingglass Theatre Company has redesigned their Studio classes for ages 2-18 years old! Take an Experiential class and open your imagination through drama, art, movement and storytelling! Come to our Technique classes, which offer the skills required to fulfill your dreams of being an actor! Move on to a Per-formance class to utilize your talents on the stage!*

Northlight Theatre Academy

Lisa Bany-Winters
9501 N. Skokie Blvd.
Skokie, IL 60077
847/679-9501 ext. 3301
www.northlight.org
lbanywinters@northlight.org

> *Five summer programs cover a wide array of topics and skills, including drama, musical theatre, improv, TV/film and backstage. The camps are offered at the N. shore Center for the Performing Arts and Evanston Township High School.*

NU Stage Theatre
Kevin Holt
Peter Chatman
500 E. 67th St.
Chicago, IL 60637
773/493-0901
www.nustagetheatre.com
> This weekly drama class meets for five months and covers everything from mime, improv and performance to audition skills.

Old Town of Folk Music
4544 N. Lincoln Ave.
Chicago, IL 60625
773/728-6000
www.oldtownschool.org
> The school offers introductory classes to theatre for young children, which can be continued in special classes that create new musicals such as Bored Silly and The Magic Zoo.

Piven Theatre Workshop
Dianna Leavitt
927 Noyes St.
Evanston, IL 60201
847/866-6597
www.piventheatre.org
> Come play at the theatre school that launched John & Joan Cusack, Aidan Quinn, Lili Taylor, Jeremy Piven and many more! Classes for young people from 4th grade through high school. Call for current class information.
> **See our ad on page 147.**

School of Performing Arts
200 E. 5th Ave., Suite 132
Naperville, IL 60563
630/717-6622
www.schoolofperformingarts.com
> The school offers a variety of theatre classes including Improv, Audition Workshop and Musical Theatre Dance Workshop.

The Second City
Jeff Gandy
1616 N. Wells St.
Chicago, IL 60614
312/664-3959
www.secondcity.com
sc1616@secondcity.com
> Second City offers a set of classes for the novice and more experienced teen improvisor.
> **See our ad on page 155.**

Steppenwolf Theatre Company
Elizabeth Levy
1650 N. Halsted St.
Chicago, IL 60614
312/335-1888 ext. 5639
www.steppenwolf.org
elevy@steppenwolf.org
> This two-semester program is led by resident artists and focuses on the creation of a new piece of work incorporating text, music, movement and visual arts.

TVI Studios
116 W. Illinois St., Suite 3E
Chicago, IL 60610
312/828-0053, 800/884-2772, ext. 3
www.tvistudios.com
> Acting and Auditioning for TV/Film/Theatre

Village Players of Oak Park
Janet Louer
1010 W. Madison St.
Oak Park, IL 60302
708/524-1892
www.village-players.org
> Digital Filmmaking
> Beginning Scene Study

Writers' Theatre
376 Park Ave.
Glencoe, IL
847/242-6007
www.writerstheatre.org
> Stories Alive; Character Play; Junior High School Ensemble; High School Ensemble

7 Training

Classes - Physical Theatre

Plasticene

2122 N. Winchester Ave., Suite 1F
Chicago, IL 60614
312/409-0400
www.plasticene.com

*Summer Physical Theatre Intensive
Ongoing Workshops*

**The Actors Gymnasium &
Performing Arts School**

Nathan Drackett
Noyes Cultural Arts Center
927 Noyes St.
Evanston, IL 60201
847/328-2795
www.actorsgymnasium.com
info@actorsgymnasium.com

*Acro-Dance, Clown Theatre, Dance 101,
Drum Performance, Gymnastics, Mime
101, The Lookingglass Workshops,
Pilates-Based Workshop, Viewpoints,
Circus Arts.*

See our ad on page 156.

Classes – Script Writing

Chicago Alliance for Playwrights
773/929-7367 ext. 60
www.chicagoallianceforplaywrights.org
info@chicagoallianceforplaywrights.org

Chicago Dramatists
1105 W. Chicago Ave.
Chicago, IL 60622
312/633-0630
www.chicagodramatists.org
newplays@chicagodramatists.org

> *Chicago Dramatists is a theatre specifically dedicated to creating and advancing new plays. They have classes in all aspects of Playwriting, from Fundamentals to Advanced. They also offer classes in Marketing, Screenwriting, Solo Performance, 10-minute plays and various weekend workshops. Chicago Dramatists has a network and resident playwright system, that helps writers develop their work.*
>
> **See our ad on page 160.**

Chicago Filmmakers Co-op
5243 N. Clark St.
Chicago, IL 60640
773/293-1447
www.chicagofilmmakers.org

> *Screenwriting 1, Screenwriting 2*

The Neo-Futurists
Sharon Greene
5153 N. Ashland Ave.
Chicago, IL 60640
773/878-4557
www.neofuturists.org
admin@neofuturists.org

> *The Neo-Futurists Performance Workshop and advanced Neo-Futurist Performance Workshop – Both workshops focus on introducing students to a new non-illusory method of writing, directing, and performing original work using their own lives and immediate environment.*

Screenwriters Group
773/665-8500
www.screenwritersgroup.com
info@screenwritersgroup.com

TBC Musical Theatre Writers Workshop
1225 W. Belmont Ave.
Chicago, IL 60657
773/929-7367
www.theatrebuildingchicago.org
allan@theatrebuildingchicago.org

> *Theatre Building Chicago's Musical Theatre Writers Workshop is dedicated to developing NEW MUSICALS and nurturing new musical theatre writers. If you are an aspiring composer, lyricist or book writer, TBC's Musical Theatre Writers Workshop is looking for YOU. The workshop begins in September. New musicals developed in the TBC Musical Theatre Writers Workshop have gone on to presentation in Boston, Chicago, Los Angeles, New York, San Diego and Seattle as well as international arenas! To learn more, download the brochure online & send completed form to the address above.*
>
> **See our ad on page 160.**

The Training Center at Victory Gardens Greenhouse
2257 N. Lincoln Ave.
Chicago, IL 60614
773/549-5788
www.victorygardens.org
information@victorygardens.org

> *As an American Center for New Plays, Victory Gardens embraces a tradition focusing on playwrights and their work. The Training Center offers workshops for experienced writers as well as opportunities for novices wishing to expand their knowledge of and experience with the craft of playwriting.*

Training

Classes - Stage Combat

Forte Stage Combat
Tim Frawley
859 Chancel Cir.
Glen Ellyn, IL 60137
630/942-9102
www.fortecombat.com
timfrawley@fortecombat.com

Piccolo Theatre
John Szostek
600 Main St.
Evanston, IL 60202
847/424-0089
www.piccolo.com
school@piccolotheatre.com

R & D Choreography
4255 N. Bernard St.
Chicago, IL 60618
847/333-1494
www.fightshop.org
info@fightshop.org

**The Actors Gymnasium &
Performing Arts School**
Nathan Drackett
Noyes Cultural Arts Center
927 Noyes St.
Evanston, IL 60201
847/328-2795
www.actorsgymnasium.com
info@actorsgymnasium.com

A variety of stage combat classes are offered. Students learn the fundamental stage combat principles of partnering, safety, and physical commitment within the context of precise, specific training. At the conclusion of the class, proficiency testing with The Society of American Fight Directors will be offered to those who qualify (no additional fee). **See our ad on page 156.**

Coaches - Acting

Bob Bills Studio
Bob Bills
650 W. Lake St., Suite 410
Chicago, IL 60661
312/928-0638
www.bobbillsstudio.com
bb@bobbillsacting.com

Bob Bills offers one-on-one monologue coaching. He can help you choose a monologue, to breathe life into your character, and to make a role-winning delivery and presentation. Check his Web site for testimonials, bios, and philosophy on acting. Discounts for multiple sessions.

Belinda Bremner
312/375-8306

Bewildered in your monologue hunt and preparation? Baffled as to how this whole business works? Monologue Mom (Belinda Bremner, AEA, SAG/AFTRA, Jefferson and Kennedy Center winner, author of Acting In Chicago, etc.) has most of the answers. Years of coaching Chicago's finest actors to the newest newcomer have produced proven solutions to audition worries and woes. Her 12 Step Program streamlines monologue selection and her direction helps you nail the piece. An expert at guiding young actors into the best university training programs, Mom is also there for you for dialects, career triage, and pretty much finishing your homework. She's home at 312/375-8306.

Dexter Bullard
dexter@plasticene.com

Dale Calandra
773/551-0875
showbizdude@aol.com

Personal Training for the Total Actor. Your Monologue is a SHOWCASE of your Talent. **Act to win!** *Contemporary, On-Camera, Classical, Commercials, Callbacks, Cold-Reading, Career Counseling. Over 1,500 coached since 1983. Creative Director: Planet iii Films, Former Artistic Director: Center Theater, Festival Theatre. A SUCCESSFUL Actor is Confident, Centered, Creative.*

Classical Training Project at Chicago Shakespeare Theatre
800 E. Grand Ave.
Chicago, IL 60611
312/595-5607
Beginning Monologue, Scene Study, Stage Combat

Linda Gillum
773/793-3077

Lori Klinka
628 Hawthorne Rd.
Frankfort, IL 60423
815/469-9846
www.loriklinka.com
lklinka@sbcglobal.net

Ruth Landis
773/732-3183
www.ruthlandis.com
ruthienergy@ruthlandis.com

Janet Louer
312/543-5297
www.janetlouer.com
janetlouer@aol.com

Ron Mace
847/727-1663
Professional Union Acting Coach. Monologues – Scene Study – Voice & Diction. 38 Years Acting Experience. 9 Year Professor with Masters Degree. All Ages – Beginners to Advanced. Call for Availability and Rates.

Richard Marlatt
773/338-8755
For beginners and seasoned professionals, work with classical and contemporary monologues, scenes, cold readings, voice and diction, and dialect training. A working professional Actors' Equity and Screen Actors Guild Actor and Director here and across the country, Richard has taught workshops and offered affordable private coaching since 1981. $45/hour.

Michael Menendian
6157 N. Clark St.
Chicago, IL 60660
773/338-2177
www.raventheatre.com
raventheatre@aol.com

Janet B. Milstein
773/465-5804
www.janetmilstein.com
act4you@msn.com
Award-winning acting instructor, Janet has trained hundreds of actors, beginners to professionals. Her students continually get cast in Chicago theatre and have been signed by agents in Chicago, NY and L.A. Janet offers affordable private coaching in monologues and cold reading that will teach you the skills to audition powerfully and with confidence. Author of 111 One-Minute Monologues, Cool Characters for Kids; Creator/Editor of the Audition Arsenal series.

Syd Moore
773/259-4275

Kurt Naebig
10 W. Hubbard St.
Chicago, IL 60610
630/495-7188

Kathryn Nash
312/943-0167
knash@ccc.edu

Monica Payne
773/878-8918
monicaannpayne@gmail.com

Fredric Stone
5040 N. Marine Dr., Suite 3A
Chicago, IL 60640
773/334-4196
fredricstone@sbcglobal.net
A working professional actor/director with 30 years experience (New York, Chicago and L.A.), he has performed with Chicago Shakespeare Theatre, Steppenwolf and Goodman among others. Fredric coaches actors in monologue and scene preparation for auditions, both contemporary and classical. He taught The Audition Workshop at Organic Theatre and currently teaches Performing Shakespeare at Victory Gardens Theatre.

Training

The Studio of the Moving Dock Theatre Company
Dawn Arnold
410 S. Michigan Ave., Suite #720
Chicago, IL 60605
312/427-5490
www.movingdock.org
contact@movingdock.org

Get expert individualized coaching for auditions or for preparing roles with Dawn Arnold, Artistic Director of The Moving Dock Theatre Company and Certified Master Teacher of the Michael Chekhov Acting Technique. Dawn's coaching gets actors into their own bodies and voices and guides them to expressive yet authentic character work. **See our ad on page 150.**

Coaches - Dialect

Martin Aistrope
4121 N. Kilbourn Ave.
Chicago, IL 60641
773/286-2862
martinaistrope@aol.com

CLEARSPEAK
Deb Kowalczyk, MA
773/255-8024
www.clearspeak.net
deb@clearspeak.net

Special expertise in modifying foreign accents and regional dialects. Dialect acquisition for the stage.

Kate DeVore
4451 N. Hamilton Ave.
Chicago, IL 60625
773/750-2030
www.TotalVoice.net

Character-based dialect acquisition and coaching for any dialect. Specific, technical coaching for sound changes, voice placement (resonance), and musicality of a dialect. Non role-specific dialect training also available, as is coaching in General American ("accent reduction"). Materials and personalized coaching tapes provided.

Coaches - Ear Prompter

Rick Plastina
1117 N. Taylor Ave.
Oak Park, IL 60302
708/386-8270
rickear@att.net

Coaches - Instrument

DePaul University – Community Music Division
804 W. Belden Ave.
Chicago, IL 60614
773/325-7262
www.music.depaul.edu

Old Town School of Folk Music
4544 N. Lincoln Ave.
Chicago, IL 60625
773/728-6000
www.oldtownschool.org

Sherwood Conservatory of Music
1312 S. Michigan Ave.
Chicago, IL 60605
312/427-6267
juth@sherwoodmusic.org

Coaches – Movement

Courtney Brown
1902 W. Addison St.
Chicago, IL 60640
773/878-3865
courtneybrownmail@yahoo.com

Chicago Center for the Alexander Technique
1252 W. Catalpa Ave.
Chicago, IL 60640
773/728-3235
www.ateducationresearch.com
ed@edbouchard.com

T. Daniel Productions
Laurie Willis
6619 N. Campbell Ave.
Chicago, IL 60645
773/743-0277
www.tdanielcreations.com

Coaches – Singing

Tamara Anderson
1023 Barberry Ln.
Round Lake Beach, IL 60073
847/546-5548
www.tamaraanderson.com
voxdoc@sbcglobal.net

Bridget Becker
773/381-9358

Deborah Bulgrin
Fine Arts Building
410 S. Michigan Ave., Studio 839
Chicago, IL 60605
773/989-1192
www.deborahbulgrin.com
bulgrintd@netzero.net

Mark Burnell
773/862-2665
markburnell.com
mark@markburnell.com

Dr. Ronald Combs
917 W. Castlewood Ter.
Chicago, IL 60640
773/271-8425
rcombs@21stcentury.net

David H. Edelfelt
Northside
Chicago, IL
773/878-SING

Matthew Ellenwood
4318 N. Sheridan Rd.
Chicago, IL 60613
773/404-2739

Gillian Kelly
773/764-0867
www.voicequestinc.com

Old Town School of Folk Music
4544 N. Lincoln Ave.
Chicago, IL 60625
773/728-6000
www.oldtownschool.org

Rebecca Patterson Voice Studio
Rebecca Patterson
773/736-6431
www.rebeccapatterson.com
xchroid1@att.net

> "My hope for voice students is that they experience freedom in their singing and enjoyment of their own artistry." Rebecca Patterson offers vocal technique for the singer and singing actor in a positive, high energy environment. Students experience expanded range and dynamics, greater power and clarity, and increased breath control.

Patricia Rusk
1263 W. Foster Ave.
Chicago, IL 60640
773/784-7875
www.par.richlogicworks.com
ruskpa@sbcglobal.net

Sherwood Conservatory of Music
1312 S. Michigan Ave.
Chicago, IL 60605
312/427-6267
www.sherwoodmusic.org
juth@sherwoodmusic.org

Peggy Smith-Okarry
1347 W. Winona St.
Chicago, IL 60640
773/728-5240

The Center For Voice
410 S. Michigan Ave., Suite 635
Chicago, IL 60605
312/360-1111

The Voice Works
312/944-3867

William Rush Voice Consultants
410 S. Michigan Ave., Suite 920
Chicago, IL 60604
773/354-6163
whrush@aol.com

Wilmette Voice & Piano Studio
847/251-7449

Coaches - Speech

Chicago Actors Studio
2040 N. Elston Ave.
Chicago, IL 60614
773/645-0222
www.actors-studio.net
chiactorsstudio@aol.com
See our ad on page 146.

CLEARSPEAK
Deb Kowalczyk, MA
773/255-8024
www.clearspeak.net
deb@clearspeak.net

> *Strongly influenced by and using techniques gleaned from Patsy Rodenburg and Kristin Linklater, Deb uses a fourfold approach to finding and freeing your true voice. Changes can be heard in the first session. The following areas are addressed: Projection, Pitch, Range, Diction, Freeing Vocal Tensions. Also treats voice disorders. Special expertise in modifying foreign accents and regional dialects. Dialect acquisition for the stage. Over 20 years experience. Individual and small group sessions are available.*

Kate DeVore
4451 N. Hamilton Ave.
Chicago, IL 60625
773/750-2030
www.totalvoice.net

> *Over 15 years experience as voice, speech and dialect coach; certified voice/speech pathologist specializing in*

> *performers' voice. Voice enhancement, exploration and development. Training in vocal projection, resonance, power, flexibility, ease and range. Vocal extremes (shouting and screaming) without injury. Vocal health and maintenance. Holistic approach to voice enhancement also available, incorporating energy and complementary healing techniques to free and strengthen the voice.*

Ron Mace
847/727-1663

> *Professional Union Voice & Diction Coach. Voice Improvement – Beginners to Advanced. Theatre – Business – Personal Enrichment. 9th Year Professor with Masters Degree. 28 Years Teaching Experience – All Ages. Call for Availability & Rates.*

Kathryn Nash
312/943-0167
knash@ccc.edu

Ann Wakefield
1500 N. LaSalle St., Suite 3C
Chicago, IL 60610
312/751-9348

William Rush Voice Consultants
410 S. Michigan Ave., Suite 920
Chicago, IL 60604
773/354-6163
whrush@aol.com

Coaches - Voice-over

Act One Studios, Inc.
Steve Merle
640 N. LaSalle St., Suite 535
Chicago, IL 60610
312/787-9384
www.actone.com
info@actone.com
> See our ad on page 142.

Acting Studio Chicago
Rachael Patterson
10 W. Hubbard St., Suite 2E
Chicago, IL 60610
312/527-4566
www.actingstudiochicago.com
info@actingstudiochicago.com
> See our ad on page 144.

Audio Producers Group
Mindy Verson
300 N.State St., Suite 3206
Chicago, IL 60610
312/220-5423
mindy@audioproducersgroup.com

Jeff Lupetin Consulting
Jeff Lupetin
847/902-4478

Sound Advice
944 N. Noble St. #1
Chicago, IL 60622
773/772-9539
www.voiceoverinfo.com
info@voiceoverinfo.com
> *Sound Advice... where the best voice-overs get their start & established talent sharpen their tools of the trade. To be successful, there's only one option... and that's Sound Advice. Visit www.voiceoverinfo.com, then call 773/772-9539*
> See our ad on page 123.

Voice Over U
Sherri Berger
773/774-9886
www.sherriberger.com
voiceoveru@sherriberger.com
> *Voice Over U is one of the most recommended voice-over training programs in the Midwest, with a complete roadmap into the business and a variety of recording workshops. Private coaching: Sherri Berger identifies trends, pinpoints a performer's strengths and weaknesses, and helps them discover more interesting vocal nuances, style and range capabilities.*

Local Universities

Columbia College
600 S. Michigan Ave.
Chicago, IL 60605
312/344-6101
www.colum.edu
etmazzocco@colum.edu
> *MFAs offered in 10 disciplines focusing on the arts, media, education, and communication.*
> See our ad on page 168.

DePaul University
2135 N. Kenmore Ave.
Chicago, IL 60614
773/325-7999
http://theatreschool.depaul.edu

> *MFAs offered in Acting, Directing, Costume Design, Lighting Design and Set Design.*

Illinois State University
School of Theatre
Campus Box 5700
Normal, IL 61761
309/438-8783
www.cfa.ilstu.edu
njeller@ilstu.edu
> *MFAs offered in Acting, Directing and Design.*

7 Training

Loyola University Chicago

Mundelein Centre 713
6525 N. Sheridan Rd.
Chicago, IL 60626
773/508-3396
www.luc.edu/theatre
theatre-info@luc.edu

Michigan State University

149 Auditorium Building
East Lansing, MI 48824
517/355-6690
www.theatre.msu.edu
theatre@msu.edu

> *MFAs offered in Acting and Production
> Design.*

Northern Illinois University

School of Theatre and Dance
Stevens Building Room 216
DeKalb, IL 60115
815/753-1335
www.niu.edu/theatre/

> *MFAs offered in Acting, Directing,
> and Design/Tech.*

Northwestern University

1949 S. Campus Dr.
Evanston, IL 60201
847/491-3170
www.communication.northwestern.edu/theatre

Roosevelt University

430 S. Michigan Ave.
Chicago, IL 60605
312/341-3719
ccpa.roosevelt.edu/theatre
theatre@roosevelt.edu

> *MFAs in Directing/Dramaturgy, Musical
> Theatre and Performance-Acting.*
> **See our ad on page 169.**

School of the Art Institute

36 S. Wabash Ave.
Chicago, IL 60603
312/345-3538
www.artic.edu
admiss@artic.edu

> *MFAs offered in Performance,
> Film, Video and New Media.*

Southern Illinois University
Department of Theatre
Carbondale, IL 62901
618/453-5741
www.siu.edu/~mcleod/
mcldpub@siu.edu
MFAs offered in Directing, Playwriting, and Design.

University of Illinois at Chicago
Deartment of Performing Arts
EPASW Bldg., 1040 W. Harrison St.
MC-255
Chicago, IL 60607
312/996-2977
www.uic.edu/depts/adpa/
dpa@uic.edu

Universty of Illinois, Urbana-Champaign
4-122 MC 072 Krannert Center
for the Performing Arts
500 S. Goodwin Ave.
Urbana, IL 61801
217/333-2371
www.theatre.uiuc.edu
MFAs offered in Acting and Design/Management/Tech.

Western Illinois University
Browne Hall
Macomb, IL 61455
309/298-1543
www.wiu.edu/theatre
MFAs offered in Acting, Directing and Design.

Speech Therapy

CLEARSPEAK
Deb Kowalczyk
773/255-8024
www.clearspeak.net
deb@clearspeak.net

Having spent 25 years as a licensed Speech Pathologist, Deb has success-fully treated all types of Speech/ Language problems. These have included, but are not limited to: Voice disorders from vocal stuttering, diction problems, language problems from stroke or head injury. Expertise with adults and children. Member of ASHA.

Kate DeVore, MA, CCC-SLP
4451 N. Hamilton Ave.
Chicago, IL 60625
773/750-2030
www.totalvoice.net

With over 15 years experience (and as a performer herself), Kate understands the unique vocal needs of performers. As a voice, speech and dialect trainer, as well as a speech pathologist special-izing in professional voice, Kate has cre-ated a unique combination of artistic and scientifically based techniques for vocal rehabilitation and speech training.

Training

Krause Speech & Language Services
233 E. Erie St., Suite 815
Chicago, IL 60611
312/943-1927
sekrause@aol.com

Kathleen E. Long
11142 S. Campbell Ave.
Chicago, IL 60655
773/239-8089

Bonnie Smith, PhD, CCC SLP
1855 W. Taylor St.
Chicago, IL 60612
312/996-6520
www.otol.uic.edu/speech.htm

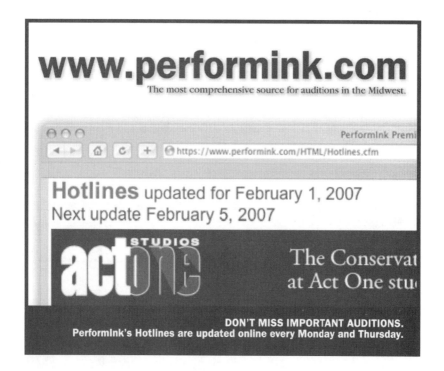

So You Want to Start a Theatre Company... Now What?

BY DON HALL

o you really want to start a theatre company? Are you sure?

This is Chicago. There is more competition for less audience than in any city in America. If your motivation is making money, you will be disappointed and discover that producing strictly for money is like any other soulless day job except you don't get vacation or insurance.

If, however, you are undaunted by the glut of existing theatre companies and the lack of a full-blown theatre audience (most of whom are in sports bars right now), then it's time to make some decisions.

- Are you starting your company to do that one show you really want to be in?
- Are you starting your company as part of a long term project that you're willing to sacrifice years of your life to maintain?

If it is the first, just go do your show and hope for the best. This article isn't for you.

For those reading who have decided that they'd like to at least attempt to climb the mountain—naked and blind—let's make some decisions, eh?

NFP or LLC?

The first decision to make is whether you want your company to be the classic nonprofit corporation or a commercial business. In the earliest stages, it won't make a huge difference but in the long run, this decision will determine a lot of your forward-moving strategies and pitfalls. Understand that a corporation is a corporation and that either style needs a board of directors, a set of bylaws, an administrative structure and genuine fiscal oversight.

The major difference between the two types center primarily on how you hope to be funded. An LLC (Limited Liability Corporation) is a commercial enter-price you pay taxes at the end of the fiscal year and you need investors to finance the whole thing. An NFP (Not For Profit) certainly allows for profit but how you fund it changes—an nfp can accept donations (no return is implied to those contributing money) and is eligible for grants (federal, municipal, and private).

To incorporate as an LLC, there are countless services available. After some research, it is recommended that you check out *www.legalzoom.com*, a company co-founded by Robert Shapiro. It has loads of information and, if you choose to use the service, has a high satisfaction rating.

To incorporate as an NFP, go to *www.nfconline.org*. The forms required are all downloadable and are fairly simple to fill out. Make sure you either a) hire a service to do this for you or b) get a professional in the field to double check your work before you apply.

Separate the Streams

You've sat around your studio apartment with your buddies and decided what kind of corporation you will be; now it's time to get into the meat of the matter. I recommend that you separate the streams (Artistic and Administrative) and maintain a certain amount of autonomy between the two. Simply put, everyone wants to be involved with the creative side and theatre administration is most often viewed as a necessary evil. Keep in mind that no matter how amazing your shows end up, without a strong and motivated business end, no one will see them.

Keep in mind one other thought: No one, when asked in second grade what he wanted to be when he grew up, answered "Arts Administrator."

There are approximately five new theatre companies that are formed in Chicago every six months. Of that five, only one will make it to a five year anniversary. The one that does has an effective administration side in the mix, one that focuses strictly on financing and board development. Ignore these aspects to be cool and bohemian and I repeat: You. Will. Fail.

Create a Game Plan

There are two statements you need to work on at this point: a Mission Statement and a Vision Statement.

The Mission is for the public to see. It is to distinguish your company from all the others in the pursuit of grants, sponsorships, and donors. Make it simple and specific; avoid the standard umbrella of, "Our theatre company is committed to creating theatre that is honest and intelligent and entertaining." No kidding, really? Specify, sweetcheeks. Is your theatre committed to presenting the works of a single playwright per season? Are you strictly a theatre for the blind? Do you present the European classics?

The Vision Statement is for your company. It is designed to map out some specifics that you don't need to waste potential donors' time with, such as the artistic arc you'll pursue and whether you have open auditions or cast internally. This may seem like a throwaway assignment, but if you take the time to create a comprehensive Vision Statement, it will save you a lot of trouble down the line— think of it as the atlas on your journey.

Now What?

You've filled out the paperwork, you have delegated both artistic and administrative authority and you've created the mission/vision for the company. Time to start fundraising and putting up shows.

Here are a few simple rules of the road to keep in mind:

PRODUCE BACKWARDS This simply means to begin each project you produce (fundraiser to show) with the end in mind. Work your calendar from the strike of your set backwards to the date of auditions and less will surprise you along the way. Remember, surprises usually cost money.

JOIN AFFILIATIONS Early on, joining professional groups will connect you to the greater network of theatre folk in town, so look into The League of Chicago Theatres and the Chicago Comedy Association (local) and The Theatre Communications Group (national).

TAKE YOUR TIME Rushing into a venture like this limits your chances of long term success in a big way, so slow down. The first couple of productions seal your reputation in the first couple of years, so make them count. Take your time and make them excellent and that ethic will repay you in kind.

The New PAV License

BY JEREMY WECHSLER

At the end of 2005, the city of Chicago established a new license for physical theatre companies. The new Performing Arts Venue (PAV) license replaced the cumbersome Public Place of Amusement (PPA) license for small theatres. The PPA was so overloaded with bureaucracy and open to corruption that many theatres avoided even trying to get one. That, however, made them vulnerable to random city shut-downs. Anyone opening a small theatre company now has no excuse not to have a PAV. In fact, many itinerant companies won't rent from a non-licensed theatre.

So, here are some basic facts about the PAV:

1. Short Shorter Shortest

The new application is only about 6 pages; survivors of the old PPA will recall its 20-plus pages with horror. As a special bonus, some of the more Byzantine requirements, such as detailed financial reporting and an extensive background check, are no longer required. You still have to get fingerprinted, but can do it at City Hall instead of that dismal police station on the S. Side.

2. "Small" Venues Only

The PAV only applies to small theatres. In this context, "small" is under 500 seats. As a special bonus, if you are performing in a church, auditorium, etc. with a larger seating capacity, you are still eligible for the PAV, providing your use of the space is incidental. That means it's shared with the church for regular services. Sadly, if you're over 1,000 seats, you still need a PPA, so I wouldn't approach the megachurches about that production of *Love! Valour! Compassion!* just yet.

3. Cheaper is Better, Right?

Even if you can't get your Alderman to waive the fee, it's much cheaper. Fifty-five dollars if you're under 500 seats. This is notably cheaper than the previous charge of $385–$500. Existing PPA venues can renew under the PAV license online if they choose. Existing "Theatrical Community Centers" will automatically renew as PAV.

4. Theatres Theatres Everywhere

Your theatre can now be located next to a church, hospital or school. Why was this forbidden before? Because the PPA covered bars and nightclubs as well as theatres. You can even put your theatre next to a residential property (R1-3 zoning). Previously, only non-profits with less than 300 seats were eligible to cozy into a residential neighborhood. This simplifies the space hunt and prevents you from having to: a) get a surveyor to figure out how far that church on the corner really is, so you could b) get a dispensation from your Alderman. Note that your physical site must still be zoned properly. You can't put your theatre into the basement of your parents' ranch house. Only next to it in an appropriate commercial or mixed-use space.

5. New Licensing Department

Previously, the Department of Revenue was in charge of PPA licensing. Now a new department, Business Affairs and Licensing, will tenderly shepherd your PAV along. Why is this good? The Department of Revenue is very, very large and had to devote a lot of resources to tracking me down about unpaid parking tickets. A smaller, more focused department can only help navigate the city licensing process. Even better, the Department of Business Affairs will assign dedicated caseworkers to track individual PAV applications. Not just one department, but one person! One phone number! One e-mail!

6. Longer Window for Reporting Management Changes

Many small theatres have a... well... shifting and dynamic board membership. Previously, you had to report these changes to the city within 10 days, and woe betide the theatre also doing a license application in that time. Now you get a comfy 60 days to report all those items.

7. The Donations Question Finally Answered

Several theatres running into PPA difficulties have attempted to request donations instead of ticket prices to avoid the PPA requirement. There was about a 15 percent success rate in this stratagem, depending on which inspector/police officer was sent to assess the situation. Now it's official. If you have under 100 seats, you can operate without a PAV. All you need is a sign (no less than a letter-sized sheet of paper) saying "Under Section 4-156-535 of the Municipal Code of Chicago, this performing arts venue may not charge an admission fee, minimum purchase requirement, membership fee, or other fee or charge imposed for the privilege of entering the premises. Any donations are purely voluntary." Catchy, no? But useful. Say you're a small theatre struggling to open your space. You finish construction and the inspectors say you have a serious problem that requires redress. They'll be back in four weeks. Your season is set to open in one. You are allowed to start your run by soliciting donations instead of tickets, which might well be less expensive than canceling your opening. All you need to open for business is the occupancy card. This is much easier to get than the PAV/PPA from an inspection standpoint and must be applied for before you start the PAV process anyway. You can easily apply for that at *www.cityofchicago.org*.

8. Theatrical Community Center, RIP

The "Theatrical Community Center" designation is replaced in its entirety by the PAV. You can no longer apply under the TCC/PPA rules. And that's a good thing. The TCC revision was an early effort to clarify some of the problems theatres faced under the PPA. All existing code on the TCC has been rolled into the new PAV.

What's the Same?

1. You still need an occupancy card. This is the placard that the city provides saying just how many people can occupy the space lawfully (if not comfortably). No placee, no performee. This is amazingly easy to get (which is a positive, as it's required to apply for the pav). It's a single page application. You need floor plans, some information about unfixed seating if you have any, and a few stamps from the zoning department. All you need to do then is schedule an inspection with the city (Mike Galvan, 312/746-9796). It takes about 45 days start to finish. You can start this process as construction is winding down.

2. Parking rules are unchanged. Spaces over 150 seats must provide one parking place for every 10 seats.

3. Pre-inspections. The Department of Buildings will still perform pre-inspections of venues to advise you about potential code violations before you sign a lease.

4. Background checks. The police background check is still required, but is "less extensive." I honestly don't know what that means, but clean up your parking tickets and be prepared to defend any previous convictions.

5. All existing fire codes and handicapped access rules. None of this changes. Not one word. Fire-retardant scenery, minimum aisle and row widths, lobby size, etc. are all still there. The PAV is meant to be easier, not a license to kill.

The PPA process was the largest operating hurdle (after money) many theatres faced. The new code provides simplicity and clarity in a much needed area for our industry.

And This Just In

As of Jan. 1, 2007, your brand-spanking-new PAV license will be good for two years. You don't have to go through the paperwork every year—just remember where you put it so you can find it in 2009.

Where Can I Get Me One?

Sadly, PAV applications are not available online, but you can apply for an occupancy card online, and you can get checklists for all of the codes required in the PAV. Go to *www.cityofchicago.org*. Click on "City Departments" at the top of the site, then scroll down to "Buildings."

To get a PAV application, you have to go to the Dept. of Business Affairs and Licensing at 121 N. LaSalle St., 8TH Floor. There, you will meet with your consultant, who will whip out an application just for you.

And that's it. Now, you just have to make sure your building is up to code. Good luck.

Theatres That Rent Rehearsal Space

A Red Orchid Theatre
1531 N. Wells St.
Chicago, IL 60610
312/943-8722
www.aredorchidtheatre.org
arot@a-red-orchid.com

Act One Studios
640 N. LaSalle St.
Chicago, IL 60610
312/787-9384
www.actone.com
info@actone.com

Acting Studio Chicago
10 W. Hubbard St., Suite 2E
Chicago, IL 60610
312/527-4566
www.actingstudiochicago.com
info@actingstudiochicago.com

Aguijon Theater Company
2707 N. Laramie Ave.
Chicago, IL 60639
773/637-5899
www.aguijontheater.org
info@aguijontheater.org

American Theater Company
1909 W. Byron St.
Chicago, IL 60613
773/929-5009
www.atcweb.org
info@atcweb.org

Annoyance Theatre
4840 N. Broadway
Chicago, IL 60640
773/561-4664
www.theannoyance.com
mike@annoyanceproductions.com

The Artistic Home
1420 W. Irving Park Rd.
Chicago, IL 60613
773/404-1100
www.theartistichome.org
theartistichome@sbcglobal.net

Athenaeum Theatre
2936 N. Southport Ave.
Chicago, IL 60657
773/935-6860
www.athenaeumtheatre.com
cfoster29@surfbest.net

Bailiwick Repertory
Bailiwick Arts Center
1229 W. Belmont Ave.
Chicago, IL 60657
773/883 1090
www.bailiwick.org
bailiwicktheater@aol.com

Blue Heron Theatre
2010 Dewey Ave.
Evanston, IL 60201
847/392-0226
blueherontheatre@wowway.com

Chase Park Theater
4701 N. Ashland Ave.
Chicago, IL 60640
773/750-7835
www.chaseparktheater.org
karenfort@earthlink.net

Chicago Actors Studio
2040 N. Elston Ave.
Chicago, IL 60622
773/735-6400
www.actors-studio.net
chiactorsstudio@aol.com

Chicago Dramatists
1105 W. Chicago Ave.
Chicago, IL 60622
312/633-0630
www.chicagodramatists.org
newplays@chicagodramatists.org

Chopin Theatre
1543 W. Division St.
Chicago, IL 60622
773/278-1500
www.chopintheatre.com
info@chopintheatre.com

City Lit Theater Co.
1020 W. Bryn Mawr Ave.
Chicago, IL 60660
773/293-3682
www.citylit.org
CityLitTheater@aol.com

Corn Productions
4210 N. Lincoln Ave.
Chicago, IL 60618
773/868-0243
www.cornservatory.org
Cornproductions@aol.com

Dominican University Center Stage
7900 W. Division St.
River Forest, IL 60305
708/488-5000
www.dom.edu/pac
dupac@dom.edu

Free Street
1419 W. Blackhawk Ave.
Chicago, IL 60622
773/772-7248
www.freestreet.org
gogogo@freestreet.org

The Gift Theatre
4802 N. Milwaukee Ave.
Chicago, IL 60630
773/283-7071
www.thegifttheatre.org
m.thornton@thegifttheatre.org

Goodman Theatre
170 N. Dearborn St.
Chicago, IL 60601
312/443-3811
www.goodmantheatre.org

Gorilla Tango Theatre
1919 N. Milwaukee Ave.
Chicago, IL 60647
773/598-4549
www.gorillatango.com
info@gorillatango.com

The GreyZelda Theatre Group
3729 N. Ravenswood Ave., Suite 138
Chicago, IL 60613
773/267-6293
www.greyzelda.com or
www.myspace.com/greyzelda
greyzeldatheatre@yahoo.com

Griffin Theatre Company
3711 N. Ravenswood Ave.
Chicago, IL 60660
773/769-2228
www.griffintheatre.com
info@griffintheatre.com

HealthWorks Theatre
2936 N. Southport Ave.
Chicago, IL 60657
773/929-4260
www.healthworkstheatre.org
info@healthworkstheatre.org

iO (Formerly Improv Olympic)
3541 N. Clark St.
Chicago, IL 60657
773/880-0199
www.iochicago.net
info@iochicago.net

Kidworks Touring Theatre Co.
5215 N. Ravenswood Ave. #307
Chicago, IL 60640
773/907-9932
www.kidworkstheatre.org
kidworkstheatre@aol.com

Lifeline Theatre
6912 N. Glenwood Ave.
Chicago, IL 60626
773/761-0667
www.lifelinetheatre.com
casting@lifelinetheatre.com

Light Opera Works
927 Noyes St., Suite 225
Evanston, IL 60201
847/869-7930
www.lightoperaworks.com
info@light-opera-works.org

Live Bait Theater
3914 N. Clark St.
Chicago, IL 60613
773/871-1212
www.livebaittheater.org
aaron@livebaittheater.org

Lookingglass Theatre Company
821 N. Michigan Ave
Chicago, IL 60611
773/477-9257
www.lookingglasstheatre.org
info@lookingglasstheatre.org

Marriott Theatre
10 Marriott Dr.
Lincolnshire, IL 60069
847/634-0204
www.marriotttheatre.com

Metropolis Performing Arts Centre
111 W. Campbell St.
Arlington Heights, IL 60005
847/577-5982
www.metropolisarts.com
info@metropolisarts.com

The Moving Dock Theatre Company
410 S. Michigan Ave., Suite 720
Chicago, IL 60605
312/427 5490
www.movingdock.org
contact@movingdock.org

The Neo-Futurists
5153 N. Ashland Ave.
Chicago, IL 60640
773/878-4557
www.neofuturists.org
info@neofuturists.org

Open Eye Productions
1800 W. Cornelia Ave., Suite 111
Chicago, IL 60657
773/510-7748
www.openeyeproductions.org
oep_rentals@yahoo.com

The Phoenix Theatre
749 N. Park Ave.
Indianapolis, IN 46202
317/635-2381
www.phoenixtheatre.org
info@phoenixtheatre.org

Piccolo Theatre
600 Main St.
Evanston, IL 60202
847/424-0089
www.piccolotheatre.com
info@piccolotheatre.com

Piven Theatre Workshop
927 Noyes St.
Evanston, IL 60201
847/866-6597
www.piventheatre.org

The Playground Theater
3209 N. Halsted St.
Chicago, IL 60657
312/961-9477
www.the-playground.com
matt@the-playground.com

Profiles Theatre
4147 N. Broadway
Chicago, IL 60613
773/549-1815
www.profilestheatre.org
profilesco@aol.com

Prop Thtr
3502-04 N. Elston Ave.
Chicago, IL 60618
773/539-7804
www.propthtr.org
info@propthtr.org

Redmoon Theatre
1438 W. Kinzie St.
Chicago, IL 60622
312/850-4430
www.redmoon.org
info@redmoon.org

Remy Bumppo Theatre Company
3717 N. Ravenswood Ave., Suite 245
Chicago, IL 60613
773/244-8119
www.remybumppo.org
info@remybumppo.org

Rogue Theater
5123 N. Clark St.
Chicago, IL 60640
773/561-5893
www.roguetheater.com
rogue@roguetheater.com

The Second City
1616 N. Wells St.
Chicago, IL 60614
312/664-4032
www.secondcity.com
sc1616@secondcity.com

the side project
1439 W. Jarvis Ave.
Chicago, IL 60626
773/973-2150
www.thesideproject.net
adam@thesideproject.net

Stage Left Theatre
3408 N. Sheffield Ave.
Chicago, IL 60657
773/883-8830
www.stagelefttheatre.com
sltchicago@stagelefttheatre.com

Steep Theatre Company
3902 N. Sheridan Rd.
Chicago, IL 60613
312/458-0722
www.steeptheatre.com
info@steeptheatre.com

Strawdog Theatre Co.
3829 N. Broadway, 2nd Floor
Chicago, IL 60613
773/528-9889
www.strawdog.org
jaz@strawdog.org

The Spot
4437 N. Broadway
Chicago, IL 60640
773/728-8933

Theatre Building Chicago
1225 W. Belmont Ave.
Chicago, IL 60657
773/929-7367
www.theatrebuildingchicago.org
boxoffice@theatrebuildingchicago.org

Theatre of Western Springs
4384 Hampton Ave.
Western Springs, IL 60558
708/246-4043
www.theatrewesternsprings.com
ad@theatrewesternsprings.com

Theo Ubique Theatre Company
1454 W. Fargo Ave., #3C
Chicago, IL 60626
773/370-0235
www.theoubique.org

TownSquare Players, Inc.
121 E. Van Buren St.
Woodstock, IL 60098
312/985-4638
www.tspin.org
Plockwoo@transunion.com

Viaduct Theatre
3111 N. Western Ave.
Chicago, IL 60618
773/296-6024
www.viaducttheatre.com
viaduct@mindspring.com

Victory Gardens Greenhouse
2257 N. Lincoln Ave.
Chicago, IL 60614
773/549-5788
www.victorygardens.org
information@victorygardens.org

Village Players Theater
1010 Madison St.
Oak Park, IL 60302
708/524-1892
village-players.org
vptmanage@yahoo.com

Virtuoso Performing Arts
8321 W. Golf Rd.
Niles, IL 60714
847/583-0740
www.virtuosoperformingarts.com
zizwiz@hotmail.com

Vittum Theater
1012 N. Noble St.
Chicago, IL 60622
773/278-7471
www.vittumtheater.org
info@vittumtheater.org

**Woodstock Musical
Theatre Company**
121 E. Van Buren St.
Woodstock, IL 60098
815/338-1789
www.woodstocktheatre.com
ohbuster95@yahoo.com

Theatres That Rent Performance Space

A Red Orchid Theatre
1531 N. Wells St.
Chicago, IL 60610
312/943-8722
www.aredorchidtheatre.org
arot@a-red-orchid.com

Apollo Theater
2540 N. Lincoln Ave.
Chicago, IL 60614
773/935-9336
www.apollochicago.com
info@apollochicago.com

Aguijon Theater Company
2707 N. Laramie Ave.
Chicago, IL 60639
773/637-5899
www.aguijontheater.org
info@aguijontheater.org

American Theater Company
1909 W. Byron St.
Chicago, IL 60613
773/929-5009
www.atcweb.org
info@atcweb.org

Annoyance Theatre
4840 N. Broadway
Chicago, IL 60640
773/561-4664
www.theannoyance.com
mike@annoyanceproductions.com

Athenaeum Theatre
2936 N. Southport Ave.
Chicago, IL 60657
773/935-6860
www.athenaeumtheatre.com
cfoster29@surfbest.net

Bailiwick Repertory
Bailiwick Arts Center,
1229 W. Belmont Ave.
Chicago, IL 60657
773/883-1090
www.bailiwick.org
bailiwick@bailiwick.org

Blue Heron Theatre
2010 Dewey Ave.
Evanston, IL 60201
847/392-0226
blueherontheatre@wowway.com

Chicago Actors Studio Theatre
2040 N. Elston Ave.
Chicago, IL 60622
773/735-6400
www.actors-studio.net
chiactorsstudio@aol.com

Chicago Dramatists
1105 W. Chicago Ave.
Chicago, IL 60622
312/633-0630
www.chicagodramatists.org
newplays@chicagodramatists.org

Chopin Theatre
1543 W. Division St.
Chicago, IL 60622
773/278-1500
www.chopintheatre.com
info@chopintheatre.com

City Lit Theater Co.
1020 W. Bryn Mawr Ave.
Chicago, IL 60660
773/293-3682
www.citylit.org
CityLitTheater@aol.com

Corn Productions
4210 N. Lincoln Ave.
Chicago, IL 60618
773/868-0243
www.cornservatory.org
Cornproductions@aol.com

Court Theatre
5535 S. Ellis Ave.
Chicago, IL 60637
773/702-7005
www.courttheatre.org
info@courttheatre.org

Dominican University Center Stage
7900 W. Division St.
River Forest, IL 60305
708/488-5000
www.dom.edu/pac
dupac@dom.edu

Free Street
1419 W. Blackhawk Ave.
Chicago, IL 60622
773/772-7248
www.freestreet.org
gogogo@freestreet.org

Goodman Theatre
170 N. Dearborn St.
Chicago, IL 60601
312/443-3811
www.goodmantheatre.org

Gorilla Tango Theatre
1919 N. Milwaukee Ave.
Chicago, IL 60647
773/598-4549
www.gorillatango.com
info@gorillatango.com

iO (Formerly Improv Olympic)
3541 N. Clark St.
Chicago, IL 60657
773/880-0199
www.iochicago.net
info@iochicago.net

Lifeline Theatre
6912 N. Glenwood Ave.
Chicago, IL 60626
773/761-0667
www.lifelinetheatre.com
casting@lifelinetheatre.com

Light Opera Works
927 Noyes St., Suite 225
Evanston, IL 60201
847/869-7930
www.lightoperaworks.com
info@light-opera-works.org

Live Bait Theater
3914 N. Clark St.
Chicago, IL 60613
773/871-1212
www.livebaittheater.org
aaron@livebaittheater.org

The Neo-Futurists
5153 N. Ashland Ave.
Chicago, IL 60640
773/878-4557
www.neofuturists.org
info@neofuturists.org

Noble Fool Theatricals
4051 E. Main St.
St. Charles, IL 60174
630/443-0438
www.noblefool.org
info@noblefool.org

The Phoenix Theatre
749 N. Park Ave.
Indianapolis, IN 46202
317/635-2381
www.phoenixtheatre.org
info@phoenixtheatre.org

Piccolo Theatre
600 Main St.
Evanston, IL 60202
847/424-0089
www.piccolotheatre.com
info@piccolotheatre.com

Piven Theatre Workshop
927 Noyes St.
Evanston, IL 60201
847/866-6597
www.piventheatre.org

The Playground Theater
3209 N. Halsted St.
Chicago, IL 60657
312/961-9477
www.the-playground.com
matt@the-playground.com

Profiles Theatre
4147 N. Broadway
Chicago, IL 60613
773/549-1815
www.profilestheatre.org
profilesco@aol.com

Prop Thtr
3502-04 N. Elston Ave.
Chicago, IL 60618
773/539-7804
www.propthtr.org
info@propthtr.org

Raven Theatre
6157 N. Clark St.
Chicago, IL 60660
773/338-2177
raventheatre.com
raventheatre@aol.com

Rogue Theater
5123 N. Clark St.
Chicago, IL 60640
773/561-5893
www.roguetheater.com
rogue@roguetheater.com

the side project
1439 W. Jarvis Ave.
Chicago, IL 60626
773/973-2150
www.thesideproject.net
adam@thesideproject.net

Stage Left Theatre
3408 N. Sheffield Ave.
Chicago, IL 60657
773/883-8830
www.stagelefttheatre.com
sltchicago@stagelefttheatre.com

Steep Theatre Company
3902 N. Sheridan Rd.
Chicago, IL 60613
312/458-0722
www.steeptheatre.com
info@steeptheatre.com

Steppenwolf Theatre Company
1650 N. Halsted St.
Chicago, IL 60614
312/335-1888
www.steppenwolf.org

Strawdog Theatre Co.
3829 N. Broadway, 2nd Floor
Chicago, IL 60613
773/528-9889
www.strawdog.org
jaz@strawdog.org

The Spot
4437 N. Broadway
Chicago, IL 60640
773/728-8933

Theatre Building Chicago
1225 W. Belmont Ave.
Chicago, IL 60657
773/929.7367
www.theatrebuildingchicago.org
boxoffice@theatrebuildingchicago.org

Theatre of Western Springs
4384 Hampton Ave.
Western Springs, IL 60558
708/246-4043
www.theatrewesternsprings.com
ad@theatrewesternsprings.com

Theo Ubique Theatre Company
1454 W. Fargo Ave., #3C
Chicago, IL 60626
773/370-0235
www.theoubique.org

Timber Lake Playhouse
8215 Black Oak Rd.
Mt. Carroll, IL 61053
815/244-2035
www.timberlakeplayhouse.org
info@timberlakeplayhouse.org

TownSquare Players, Inc.
121 E. Van Buren St.
Woodstock, IL 60098
312/985-4638
www.tspinc.org
Plockwoo@transunion.com

Trap Door Theatre
1655 W. Cortland Ave.
Chicago, IL 60622
773/384-0494
www.trapdoortheatre.com
trap_door@earthlink.net

Viaduct Theatre
3111 N. Western Ave.
Chicago, IL 60618
773/296-6024
www.viaducttheatre.com
viaduct@mindspring.com

Victory Gardens Greenhouse
2257 N. Lincoln Ave.
Chicago, IL 60614
773/549-5788
www.victorygardens.org
information@victorygardens.org

Village Players Theater
1010 Madison St.
Oak Park, IL 60302
708/524-1892
www.village-players.org
vptmanage@yahoo.com

Vittum Theater
1012 N. Noble St.
Chicago, IL 60622
773/278-7471
www.vittumtheater.org
info@vittumtheater.org

**Woodstock Musical
Theatre Company**
121 E. Van Buren St.
Woodstock, IL 60098
815/338-1789
www.woodstocktheatre.com
ohbuster95@yahoo.com

Costume & Makeup Supplies

A Magical Mystery Tour
6010 W. Dempster St.
Morton Grove, IL 60053
847/966-5090

All Dressed Up Costumes
150 S. Water St.
Batavia, IL 60510
630/879-5130
www.alldressedupcostumes.com

Beatnix
3400 N. Halsted St.
Chicago, IL 60657
773/281-6933

Beverly Costume Shop
11628 S. Western Ave.
Chicago, IL 60643
773/779-0068

Broadway Costumes, Inc.
1100 W. Cermak Rd.
Chicago, IL 60608
312/829-6400
www.broadwaycostumes.com
info@broadwaycostumes.com

Center Stage
503 Rt. 59
Aurora, IL 60504
630/851-9191
www.mycenterstage.com
centerstagecostume@sbcglobal.net

Chicago Costume Company
1120 W. Fullerton Ave.
Chicago, IL 60614
773/528-1264
www.windycitycostume.com
chicagocostume@gmail.com

Facemakers, Inc.
140 Fifth St.
Savanna, IL 61074
815/273-3944
www.facemakersincorporated.com

Fantasy Costumes
4065 N. Milwaukee Ave.
Chicago, IL 60641
773/777-0222
www.fantasycostumes.com

**Josie O'Kain Costume
& Theatre Shop**
2419B W. Jefferson St.
Joliet, IL 60435
815/741-9303
www.josieokain.com

Kryolan
132 Ninth St.
San Francisco, CA 94103
800/KRY-OLAN
www.kryolan.com
info-usa@kryolan.com

MAC
40 E. Oak St.
Chicago, IL 60611
312/951-7310
www.maccosmetics.com

Sephora
www.sephora.com

Stage and Theatre Makeup
www.stageandtheatremakeup.com

Stage Supply
www.stagesupply.com

Theatrical Shop
www.theatricalshop.com

Lighting Rental

Chicago Spotlight, Inc.
1658 W. Carroll Ave.
Chicago, IL 60612
312/455-1171
www.chicagospotlight.com

Designlab
328 N. Albany Ave.
Chicago, IL 60612
773/265-1100
www.designlab-chicago.com
doug@dlabchicago.net

Grand Stage Lighting Company
630 W. Lake St.
Chicago, IL 60661
312/332-5611
www.grandstage.com

PR Firms

Carol Fox & Associates
1412 W. Belmont Ave.
Chicago, IL 60657
773/327-3830
www.carolfoxassociates.com

Noreen Heron and Associates
2227 N. Southport Ave.
Chicago, IL 60614
773/477-7666
www.heronpr.com
nheron@heronpr.com

Kensey Communications
Barbara Kensey
kenseycomm@sbcglobal.net

Margie Korshak, Inc.
875 N. Michigan Ave., Suite 1535
Chicago, IL 60611
312/751-2121

PitBull PR
2131 W. Culyer Ave.
Chicago, IL 60618
773/879-4610

The Silverman Group
Beth Silverman
1 E. Superior St., Suite 405
Chicago, IL 60611
312/932-9950
www.silvermangroupchicago.com

Tree Falls Productions
Karin McKie
773/856-6767
karin@treefalls.com

Prop Shops

Broadway Costumes, Inc.
1100 W. Cermak Rd.
Chicago, IL 60608
312/829-6400
www.broadwaycostumes.com
info@broadwaycostumes.com

Chicago Costume Company
1120 W. Fullerton Ave.
Chicago, IL 60614
773/528-1264
www.windycitycostume.com
chicagocostume@gmail.com

Chicago Scenic Studios, Inc.
1315 N. Branch St.
Chicago, IL 60622
312/274-9900
www.chicagoscenic.com
info@chicagoscenic.com
Drapery, Backdrops.

Fantasy Costumes
4065 N. Milwaukee Ave.
Chicago, IL 60641
773/777-0222
www.fantasycostumes.com

Lost Eras
1511 W. Howard St.
Chicago, IL 60626
888/74PROPS
www.losteras.com
losteras@sbcglobal.net
*Costume and Props sales and rentals.
15,000 Sq. Ft. – 2 Levels jam packed.
Over 1,000,000 pcs of clothing in
stock at all times. Vintage costumes –
Theatrical – Halloween. 1,000s of wigs,
masks, makeup, mascots. Complete
set rental and constuming for period
films. Student film and school discounts.
Expert assistance to help you find
every-thing you need. We've been cos-
tuming tv, movie, theatre & parties for
over 30 years. No production too big
or too small... come on in!*

Prop Art, Ltd.
Mary Burzynski, Art Director
1535 N. Western Ave.
Chicago, IL 60622
773/227-6755
www.prop-art.com
Mary@prop-art.com
No rentals; custom models and props.

Prop Mart, Inc.
2343 W. Saint Paul Ave.
Chicago, IL 60647
773/772-7775

PROPabilities, Inc.
1517 N. Elston Ave.
Chicago, IL 60622
773/278-2384
No costumes, just props.

Ravenswood Studio, Inc.
5645 N. Ravenswood Ave.
Chicago, IL 60660
773/769-4100
www.ravenswoodstudio.com

Tamara Backdrops
3121 N. Rockwell St.
Chicago, IL 60618
773/596-5588
www.backdrops.com
backdrops@backdrops.com

Three Sisters Antique Mall
13042 S. Western Ave.
Blue Island, IL 60406
708/597-3331

Zap Props
3611 S. Loomis Pl.
Chicago, IL 60609
773/376-2278
www.zapprops.com
zapprops@sbcglobal.net

Stage Weapons

Arms and Armor
1101 Stinson Blvd. NE
Minneapolis, MN 55413
612/331-6473
www.armor.com

IAR Arms
33171 Camino Capistrano
San Juan Capistrano, CA 92675
877/722-1873
www.iar-arms.com
sales@iar-arms.com

The Armoury American Fencers Supply
1180 Folsom St.
San Francisco, CA 94103
415/863-7911
www.amfence.com
amfence@amfence.com

Thrift Stores

Ark Thrift Shop
 1302 N. Milwaukee Ave.
 Chicago, IL 60622
 773/862-5011
 www.arkchicago.org

Ark Thrift Shop
 3345 N. Lincoln Ave.
 Chicago, IL 60657
 773/248-1117
 www.arkchicago.org

Brown Elephant Resale
 3651 N. Halsted St.
 Chicago, IL 60657
 773/549-5943

Disgraceland
 3338 N. Clark St.
 Chicago, IL 60657
 773/281-5875

Kismet Vintage Clothing and Furniture
 2923 N. Southport Ave.
 Chicago, IL 60657
 773/528-4497

Ragstock
 812 W. Belmont Ave.,
 2nd Flr & Basement
 Chicago, IL 60657
 773/868-9263
 www.ragstock.com

Salvation Army Thrift Store
 773/477-1771
 www.salvationarmy.org
   There are more than 20 Salvation Army stores in Chicago. Visit their Web site to find a convenient location.

Threads
 2327 N. Milwaukee Ave.
 Chicago, IL 60622
 773/276-6411
 www.threadsetcresale.com
 theads@theadsetcresale.com

Unique Thrift Store
 3000 S. Halsted St.
 Chicago, IL 60608
 312/842-0942

White Elephant Shop
 2380 N. Lincoln Ave.
 Chicago, IL 60614
 773/883-6184

The Jeff Awards

BY CARRIE L. KAUFMAN

n 1968, four actors, at the behest of Actors' Equity, looked for a way to honor actors in Chicago. They came up with an annual award, and decided to name it after the celebrated 19TH century actor Joseph Jefferson III, who made his home in Chicago when not touring the country playing Rip Van Winkle. In October of 1969, the newly formed Jeff Committee gave out six awards to seven Equity theatres. In 1973, non-Equity theatres were added to the judging. Three citations were given that first year. Now, the Equity and Citations wings of the Jeffs encompass over 50 producing organizations each at any given time. The latest Equity Awards included 28 categories; while the 2006 non-Equity Citations had 25 categories.

A Bit About the Committee

The Jeff Committee is a 45-plus member group made up of current and former theatre professionals, arts writers, theatre instructors, professors, arts administrators, and a few lawyers with strong backgrounds in theatre. There are stringent requirements to get on the committee and the commitment each member must make is incredible.

Every month, committee members must submit 12 days that they are free to go to opening nights. Then, during the runs of shows, each committee member must see 75 percent of the shows that are recommended. This means that Jeff Committee members go to the theatre four to five nights a week—sometimes more during September and January.

Members are also held to strict conflict of interest requirements. If there is even a perception of a conflict, a member must recuse him or herself from judging a particular production or theatre or actor. Failure to even turn in a conflict of interest statement can result in expulsion from the committee.

One criticism of the Jeff Committee is that it is made up of middle-aged, or older, people. That's pretty much true, but not for lack of trying. Younger theatre professionals often don't often have the time to commit, even though the committee is constantly trying to recruit new blood.

There are about 40 theatre professionals in Chicago that do participate in the Jeffs judging, with a lot less time commitment. They're the members of the Arts & Technical (A/T) Team. Two A/T Team members are assigned to judge an opening night, along with five Jeff Committee members. The A/T Team impacts whether or not a show gets recommended, but has no vote after opening night.

So, What Do I Have to Do to Get a Jeff?

Ah, yes, the requirements for Jeff eligibility are quite Byzantine, but ruthlessly fair. Let's just say that in order for a show to be Jeff eligible, each of the seven opening night judges must pull a lever that will trigger a ball to slide down a fluted ramp at a 70 degree angle for six feet till it hits an alarm bell that wakes up a parrot that flies to each of the committee members and tells them which shows to go see.

Confused? OK, here are the real requirements.

Equity theatres are eligible to be judged the moment they open their doors. They must notify the committee in writing that they are requesting judges by the 18th of the month before the month in which opening night is to occur. Each production must run for a minimum of 18 performances over three weeks, and one of those can't be a weekday matinee. There also must be at least one performance on each weekend of the run.

Equity theatres also must be located within a 30 mile radius of the intersection of State and Madison in downtown Chicago.

Non-Equity eligibility requirements are pretty similar, with a couple of differences. The main one is that non-Equity theatres must have been in existence for two consecutive years, and produced at least two shows in each of those years, before they can be Jeff eligible. Each of the shows produced during that two-year period must have had at least nine performances.

Another difference is that non-Equity theatres must be located in the city of Chicago to be eligible (Circle Theatre in Forest Park has been grandfathered in), and must be incorporated as a not-for profit. For-profit, non-Equity companies are not Jeff eligible.

Non-Equity companies also must perform 18 shows, but they have to do it in a minimum of four weeks, not three as with Equity shows. One of the performances must be a Friday, Saturday or Sunday of each week, and matinees don't count. Non-Equity theatres must also notify the committee that they'll need judges by the 18th of the month prior to the opening month.

The Jeff Committee has recently expanded its categories to include solo performance in the Equity (Awards) wing, and musical theatre in the non-Equity (Citations) wing. The committee aims to be more fluid, but there are certain categories that are not judged at this time. They are: late-night (after 9:30 p.m.), puppet theatre, opera, performance art (as opposed to solo performance), children's theatre, student or youth theatre, foreign language theatre, mime, unscripted or improvised theatre and staged readings.

The only other rule worth noting here is that theatres are required to give Jeff Committee members tickets to see their shows. For Equity theatres, members may request no more than two tickets per show. For non-Equity theatres Jeff Committee members can only be given one free ticket per show, with a limit of 40 tickets that tho thoatro has to oot aoido por produotion. If a Joff judgo wanto to bring hio wifo or partner to a non-Equity show, he has to pay for that extra person.

There are other rules about revivals, multiple plays, repertory, etc. A full rundown can be found on the Jeffs Web site at *www.jeffawards.org*. Judge request forms can also be found online.

But How do I Get Recommended?

Seven judges—five committee members and two A/T Team members—are randomly assigned to go to opening night of a show. Judges are limited to one opening per theatre per season. The judges call in their votes by 9 a.m. the next morning and, if they liked your show, it's recommended. If a show is recommended, the rest of the Jeff Committee has to see it. A recommended show does not guarantee a nomination, but theatres have found that it does help with marketing.

There are a number of ways that a theatre can make the grade to a Jeff recommendation.

For **Equity productions**, a show may be recommended if:

There are positive votes from at least 5 judges **+** *at least 4 of the judges vote for the same element (directing, ensemble, lighting, etc.)* **+** *at least 3 judges agree on a second element*

~ OR ~

There are 20 or more votes from at least 5 judges.

~ OR ~

All 7 judges vote for the same element.

For Equity productions with fewer than four actors, the second element requirement is waived.

For **non-Equity** productions, a show may be recommended if:

There are positive votes from at least 5 judges. **+** *At least 4 judges vote for the same element.* **+** *At least 3 judges vote for the same second element.*

~ OR ~

There are 5 votes for a single element **+** *2 votes for the same second element.*

~ OR ~

There are 6 votes for a single element **+** *one vote for a second element.*

~ OR ~

All 7 judges vote for the same element.

~ OR ~

There are 15 or more votes from at least 5 judges.

For productions with fewer than 4 actors, only one element needs to receive at least 4 votes.

Got that?

Getting Nominated

At the end of the Jeff season (April 1–March 31 for non-Equity; August 1–July 31 for Equity), all the votes are tabulated. Speaking generally, the top vote-getters in each category receive nominations and go on the final ballot. While the Jeff Committee seeks to have five nominees in each category, the statistics used are more complicated.

For instance, say Actor A received votes on 80% of the ballots cast by the Jeff judges during the run of his show, Actor B on 76%, Actor C on 72% and Actor D (the next highest vote getter) on 48%. In this case, even though Actor D was one of the top five vote-getters, he will not be nominated, and there will be only three nominees in this category. Similarly, suppose Designers A, B, C and D all received votes on more than 80% of their ballots, Designer E got 77%, Designer F got 75% and Designer G got 74%. In that case, Designers E, F and G are considered to be in a statistical tie, so all three would appear on the final ballot, leading to seven nominees in that category. In the end, though, you can be assured that each of the nominees received enough votes that they have a chance of winning an award or citation.

Narrowing it Down

Figuring out the winner is different for each wing of the Jeff Committee. Nominations and recipients for both Equity and Citations are based on percentages, not numbers of votes. The percentage is determined by dividing the number of votes received by the number of judges attending the production. This eliminates any advantage or disadvantage when different productions are seen by different numbers of Jeff members.

For Equity productions, each Jeff judge receives a ballot with the nominees in each category. A Jeff judge may only vote on a category if he or she has seen more than half of the nominees. Each judge receives as many votes as they've seen productions in the category. For instance, if Jeff judge A has seen four of the nominees for Outstanding Production, she has four votes to distribute. She could put all four towards one nominee, divide them among two or three, or give one vote to each production she saw. Each judge fills out his or her ballot, and the results are tabulated. The nominee with the most votes receives the Award.

The only exceptions to this process occur in the New Work and Adaptation categories, which are non-competitive. Then, in a manner similar to choosing nominees, one or more productions could receive the Award.

The non-Equity Citations are completely non-competitive, which means there can be more than one recipient in each category. They are so non-competitive, in fact, that the committee doesn't use the word "winners." Each Jeff judge receives a ballot and simply checks off as many nominees in each category as he or she considers deserving. The determination of the final recipients is similar to that used to determine nominees, and one, two or even all of the nominees in a category could receive Citations.

All awards are inherently subjective and are therefore open to criticism. The Jeffs certainly get their share. But the complicated rules, and the rigor with which they're enforced, assure that the human element is taken out of the process as much as possible. In the end, the Jeff Citations and Awards are a wonderful celebration of Chicago theatre. And Chicago theatre is richer for the dedication of the Jeff Committee members.

Biographies

Christina Biggs is a freelance writer whose work has appeared on stage and in print. Most recently, she has worked on the children's musicals *Fu Manchu Tied Up My Mom*, *The Adventures of Anansi the Spider*, *Ma Liang's Magic Paintbrush* and *The Reluctant Dragon*. Christina has worked as an editor for STAGEBILL MAGAZINE and the CHICAGO THEATER GUIDE, and currently writes for publications such as PERFORMINK and the CHICAGO TRIBUNE.

Becky Brett has been a regular contributor to PERFORMINK since 2000. She is the executive producer of 10 to Midnight Productions, an event planning company with a performing arts focus. She is also active in the theatre community, working with the Chicago Improv Festival and as a company member for Appetite Theatre.

Jen Ellison is the artistic director of WNEP Theater and has worked as a freelance director, actor and writer in Chicago for the last 10 years. Jen has been involved in the last three editions of THE BOOK: AN ACTOR'S GUIDE TO CHICAGO and has served as ad manager, co-editor and project manager.

Arlo Bryan Guthrie designs advertising, collateral, and online materials for an assortment of industries, including Chicago theatre. He served as the Marketing Manager for Defiant Theatre (R.I.P.) for five years. He is not related to the famous Arlo Guthrie; his parents were merely too young to name children. *www.arlodesign.com*

Jenn Q. Goddu is a freelance journalist covering primarily theatre and the arts. She reviews regularly for the CHICAGO READER and is a frequent contributor to the CHICAGO TRIBUNE, PERFORMINK, AOL CHICAGO and other regional publications. Her writing has also been published in AMERICAN THEATER and PLAYBILL. She is a member of the American Theatre Critics Association.

Don Hall is the Founding Director of WNEP Theater and was the executive director of WNEP for 14 years. Don is also an actor, director, writer, teacher, and has produced over 70 original plays, musicals, improvisations and performance art pieces over the past 18 years in Chicago.

Carrie L. Kaufman is the editor and publisher of PERFORMINK, Chicago's theatre and film trade paper for almost 20 years. She is the recipient of two Lisagor Awards for Exemplary Journalism and a Jeff Citation for PERFORMINK's service to the Chicago theatre community. Carrie also writes and performs performance poetry and monologues, and has been known to pen a lyric or two.

Dave Stinton is a cartoonist and caricaturist who drew "The Blackbox" for PERFORMINK from 2002 through 2005. He was also Playwright in Residence for WNEP Theater from 2003 through 2005, having co-written *The Mysteries of Harris Burdick*, *Dirty Bible Stories*, and *Let There Be Light* (2004 New York International Fringe Festival selection).

Jeremy Wechsler is the founder and artistic director of Theater Wit, which dedicates itself to producing plays of humor and intelligence. Jeremy has been chronicling Theater Wit's search for a space of its own in the pages of PERFORMINK—a saga that will likely continue till the next edition of THE BOOK. If you are so interested in Jeremy that you're reading his bio right now, then visit *www.theaterwit.org* for tons more trivia.

Index

Advertiser's Index